David Boyle has been writing about new ideas for more than a quarter of a century. He is co-director of the New Weather Institute, a fellow of the New Economics Foundation, has stood for Parliament and is a former independent reviewer for the Cabinet Office. He is the author of *Alan Turing, Scandal* and *Before Enigma,* as well as a range of other historical studies. He lives in the South Downs.

Lost at Sea

The story of the
USS *Indianapolis*

David Boyle

THE REAL PRESS
www.therealpress.co.uk

Published in 2016 by the Real Press (Kindle edition by
Endeavour Press. www.therealpress.co.uk
© David Boyle

The moral right of David Boyle to be identified as the
author of this work has been asserted in accordance
with the Copyright, Designs and Patents Acts of 1988

ISBN (print) 978-1533131546

For Caroline

Contents

Introduction

A multi-faceted tragedy – with sharks

"We returned to our loved ones, but we were never the same again. Most were markedly changed. Young boys had become mature older men, aged beyond their years. All because of those days in the sea."
Harlan Twible, survivor, quoted in Doug Stanton's book *In Harm's Way*

On the third day he spent in the middle of the Pacific Ocean, held up by nothing more than a life jacket that was rotting in fuel oil, without having eaten and drunk anything since he had leapt off his ship, Zeb Wilcox was woken up by a bump against his legs.

He had been dozing, barely conscious in the searing heat of the day and the freezing cold of the night. He woke with a start and a rush of adrenalin, afraid that it was late afternoon – because that seemed to be feeding time for the tiger sharks and oceanic whitetip sharks which had been circling the men in the water for days.

He had the impression he was being pulled under water and he fought for his life. Coming to the surface he saw two large grey-coloured sharks staring at him. They were about ten feet away and were at least ten feet long. "I think they were trying to see if I was dead so they could eat me," he wrote later.

Wilcox was from Texas. He had only just come off duty and laid down on the top deck of the cruiser *Indianapolis* in the warm night when two huge explosions seemed to tear the ship almost in two. By the time he had found his lifejacket, the *Indianapolis* was leaning so heavily that he found himself literally stepping into the water. By doing so, he had become one of the 900 or so men who had escaped, many of them wounded, as the ship disappeared beneath the waves just twelve minutes after being hit by two torpedoes from a Japanese submarine. By the bump in the night, their numbers had probably dwindled to fewer than 400 and more would die during the day, though help was about, finally, to be on its way. But not before the sharks had found them,

"I said to them: 'You don't bother me and I won't bother you'." Then, realising that he had drifted away from his friends, he kicked off and swam between his two visitors to go back to them, and they followed him, bemused perhaps, all the way.

Whether the sharks which circled the men in the water ate the living, as some of the reports of screams and sudden disappearances suggested, or whether they confined themselves to the dead, was just one of the many controversies that continue to this day. But most authorities agree that the feeding frenzy on the survivors of the *Indianapolis* may have been the biggest shark attack of its kind in modern history. Whatever the truth, only 316 of the crew of nearly 1,200 survived. Their story was remembered in the film *Jaws* and in hearings in the US Senate a generation later, initiated by a schoolboy – leading to the exoneration of *Indianapolis'* wronged captain.

The fact that we know so much about what happened immediately after the sinking is down largely to the ship's doctor Lewis Haynes, who dictated a long account between sleeps, within days of his rescue. It is right that this book about *Indianapolis* should focus on the loss and rescue. But the story of this ship goes beyond that, because it was not just the ship that disappeared; it was also one of the most famous ships of the twentieth century. This short book tells its tale.

The few ships in history that were never seen again, even if that only seemed the case for a little while, have gone down in history as ships that disappeared. The *Marie Celeste* reappeared of course in 1872, but without her crew. Nobody knows what became of John Cabot's expedition fleet of four ships, not seen since 1498, and for a long time Sir John Franklin's expedition to the North West Passage seemed to have disappeared into thin ice.

More recently, ships that disappeared tended to be in the vast expanses of the southern oceans: the SS *Baychimo,* adrift since 1931. The Australian submarine AE1 on its way on the long journey north in 1914. The Australian cruiser *Sydney* in 1941. *Indianapolis* was one of these, perhaps the most regal of them all – former fleet flagships very rarely disappear, after all – yet for five days at the tail end of the Second World War, she had effectively been wiped off the map.

The story of how that happened, and how the few that remained of her crew were eventually rescued from mid-Pacific, have become one of the most enduring – and notorious – of wartime sea stories. But the meaning of the *Indianapolis* goes beyond a simple sinking. What makes the story of this American warship so compelling is that it means so many things. It means the flagship of the fighting admiral Raymond Spruance, in 1943-44, during the crucial battles to control the central Pacific.

It means the delivery of the key components of the first atomic bomb dropped in anger, in this case on Hiroshima.

It means the greatest single loss of life at sea in an American naval disaster at war.

It means the gruelling, heroic and desperate struggle to survive of the crew, the biggest attack by sharks on human beings ever recorded, and the tragic suicide of the captain – and the campaign by a school pupil to clear his name three decades later.

It also means the cover-up by the naval authorities about what had gone wrong, and why the crew had been inadvertently left to die.

This book is designed to interweave all these themes to provide a short and informative, and above all, readable, guide to the *Indianapolis* story. But to tell the intertwined tales also of the two men at the heart of the story: Captain Charles McVay and the man who sank the ship, Mochitsura Hashimoto.

But it also looks more closely at the peculiar consequences of inter-service rivalries in wartime, and what happens when deference and protocol drives out common sense.

Chapter 1
A regal ship

I wish to have no Connection with any Ship that does not Sail fast for I intend to go in harm's way."
John Paul Jones, 1778

There was something beautiful about cruisers in the twentieth century. They were sleek and fast as they carved through the waves ahead of the fleet, the workhorses of navies all over the world, in the days when they were designed to be the eyes and ears of the admirals at the heart of the battle lines. Even now, we remember them as smoky, buffeted and bold, storming through the north Atlantic – or white and presidential, wandering from port to port through the Americas. And of all the great cruisers, *Norfolk, Exeter, Emden, Caroline, Indianapolis* was perhaps the most famous, though her rakish lines changed often as the technology accelerated ahead in the years of the Second World War.

The problem for cruisers was that, as technology changed naval warfare, they were destined to lose their role – the last cruisers were launched in the 1960s, and it was by then unclear quite what they were for. But four decades before that, at the end of the 1920s, cruisers were the very measure of modern warfare. The number of cruisers a nation possessed was still not quite as important as the number of ships of the line, but it was a vital way of assessing the strength of a nation and the heart of the problem of the naval arms race.

Then, in 1929, the Wall Street Crash had catapulted the developed nations into the foothills of the Great Depression and undermined the budgets which was going to pay for those navies. The string of naval treaties that characterised those years became more urgent as the Depression bit. But when the Geneva Conference broke up in 1927, having failed to restrict the size of the world's navies, President Calvin Coolidge had signed a bill that turbo-charged American warship building to bring the US navy up to the same size as the British, in a programme that included fifteen new light cruisers.

One of these was to be *Indianapolis*. In fact, before she was more than a few rivets on the ground, *Indianapolis* was redesignated as a heavy cruiser, by virtue of her eight-inch gun main armament, because the definition changed as a result of the London Naval Treaty of 1930. She was also designed to have a weight pushing upwards towards the 'heavy' definition of 10,000 tons, though in fact *Indianapolis* never quite reached that limit.

The truth was that, actually, light cruisers were losing their main function – as the eyes of the fleet, riding out miles ahead of the main battlefleet and its squadrons of battleships. There were now carrier planes to do that job, and there would soon be radar too. Light cruisers were to find a new role as anti-aircraft platforms before disappearing from Jane's Fighting Ships entirely but, for the war that was to come, they would still form the backbone of the embattled navies.

But what was the function of a heavy cruiser? These were originally designed to have a major fighting capacity in their own right, able to take on surface raiders, to patrol the ports of far-flung empires, to impress and to guard sea lanes in a way that vulnerable battleships could not. What the US navy did, which the more conservative admirals in Britain did not, was to use their manoeuvrable and fast cruisers as flagships. In the Royal Navy, admirals still struggled along on their own admiral's bridge above the captains of the most powerful modern battleships. The US admirals were more far-sighted in this, and much else besides. When Roosevelt met Churchill in mid-Atlantic in 1941, Churchill came in the battleship *Prince of Wales,* but Roosevelt chose to be transported in the cruiser *Augusta.*

It was the American way. Their fighting admirals of the Second World War would sweep from island to island on cruisers. And no cruiser apart from *Indianapolis* would have such experience as a flagship.

It is the launch of a ship, when it enters the water, speeded on by a bottle of champagne broken across the bows, which is usually considered to be its moment of birth. *Indianapolis* was launched on 7 November 1930 by Lucy Taggart, daughter of a former mayor of Indianapolis in Camden, New Jersey. Now a broken backwater of the most exhausting urban decay, Camden was then a vital outpost of the New York Shipbuilding Company on the Delaware River.

Like the light cruisers that she started as, *Indianapolis* was designed for a top speed of nearly 33 knots, unusual for a ship of that size. And in size and appearance, she perhaps resembled most the slightly newer British cruiser *Belfast*, which can still be wandered around next to Tower Bridge in the Pool of London. Like *Belfast*, the space between her two rakish funnels was given over to a seaplane and crane to hoist it in and out of the ocean. Before radar, this was the real eyes of the fleet. Like *Belfast*, she was also given the pennant number CA-35 (*Belfast* was C35).

Indianapolis was classified as a 'Portland' class cruiser, though there were only two of that kind ever build. The 'Portland' class was the third class of US cruisers built following the design stipulations of the Washington Naval Treaty in 1922. Below the waterline, she had 21 watertight compartments and a belt of armour to protect against shellfire and torpedoes of between two and five inches thick. She had four propellers, four turbines to drive them, fuelled by eight boilers. The result was 107,000 shaft horse power and a speed designed for 32.7 knots. Her first sea trials led to complaints that she rolled badly in heavy weather.

Both *Indianapolis* and *Portland* were equipped to be fleet flagships, so that they required a basic crew of 807 in peacetime but could increase that to 1,229 when they were operating as fleet flagships in wartime and needed to accommodate all the admiral's staff. Even a crew of over 800 was like a small town and the ships were equipped with a water desalination plant, a tailor, a butcher, a laundry, a bakery and a dentist.

The first commanding officer of *Indianapolis*, John Smeallie, took her to sea early in 1932. It was the month of Gandhi's arrest by the British and the refusal of the Roosevelt administration to recognise the Japanese government imposed on Manchuria. As Hitler was gearing up for power, *Indianapolis* sped into the Atlantic and into Guantanamo Bay in Cuba before going through the Panama Canal and down the coast of Chile.

The first of the ship's important visitors was about to make use of the services of *Indianapolis*, and she was in Maine in the summer of 1933 to fetch the newly-elected president Franklin Roosevelt to take him south to Annapolis with six members of his new cabinet. Roosevelt was a former assistant secretary to the navy. He chose his ships with care and some background knowledge. Not for nothing was *Indianapolis* equipped with a teak quarter deck and a luxurious admiral's barge.

In September, it was back to work carrying the great and good, in this case the Navy Secretary

Claude Swanson to inspect the navy in the Pacific, and on to Hawaii. It was there, on 1 November 1933 – the day that the regulations for Dachau concentration camp were first put into effect – that Indianapolis first became a flagship, in this case of Scouting Group 1. She stayed as flagship until 1941, with brief interludes taking Roosevelt to naval reviews – or, in 1936, taking him on a goodwill tour of Brazil, Argentina and Uruguay. Roosevelt sat in his wheelchair at the stern of the white ship he had chosen to transport him, the flagship of the navy's scouting fleet.

The Japanese know the period of militarism and war which ended with their surrender in 1945 as *kurai tanima,* or the 'dark valley'. But the roots of the war in the Pacific go back to a dark valley brought about by the same Wall Street Crash which nearly meant that *Indianapolis* was never built.

When Roosevelt was sailing down the coast of Latin America in *Indianapolis*, he was considering the effects of devaluing the dollar. He was then engaged in a desperate race for recovery without worrying about the effect it might have on other countries. Countries without their own raw materials, like Japan and Germany, suffered more than most.

Japan had been modernising at great speed. In the 80 years since Commodore Perry's American fleet steamed into a reluctant Tokyo Harbour, bringing world trade to the Japanese, they had turned themselves into a major trading force and a formidable military power - defeating the Russian Fleet at the Battle of Tsushima in 1905, with a British admiral taking notes from a deckchair on the Japanese flagship.

But unlike Germany and Italy, there was no sudden seizure of power by an absolute dictator: Japan drifted slowly towards authoritarianism. The emperor was too aloof for day-to-day decision-making – presiding in silence over the great councils of state – and this power vacuum allowed militaristic thinking in the army to become increasingly influential. This, and the way the international economy was sucking the life out of Japan's new-found wealth, was enough to let a group of middle-ranking officers take over the nation.

In September 1931, some of these officers in the Kwantung Army, guarding the South Manchurian railway, attacked the Chinese garrison in Mukden. A small bomb had exploded there – probably planted by Japanese agents – and they used this as a pretext to take control of what they claimed was a dangerous security situation. But within the next few months they had begun the process of taking control of the whole of Manchuria, which they turned into the puppet state of Manchukuo – with the former Chinese emperor Henry P'u Yi, the so-called *Last Emperor*, on the throne. When furious crowds attacked Japanese people in Shanghai in protest, the city was bombed from the air for six weeks. The League of Nations protested but it made no difference: Japan resigned in 1933.

More importantly, the officers responsible for the original Mukden attack were never censored by Tokyo, and the army realised it could do what it liked. When the guerrilla war with Mao Tse-tung's communists made it seem necessary to push south in China, there was nobody in Tokyo to deny them permission, and in the following year they were moving into China itself, shocking the world with stories of bombing civilians, rape and torture.

Then, in February 1936, the fanatics struck. Officers in the First Infantry Division suddenly attacked and killed a long list of some of the most influential liberal people in Japanese society, seizing the prime minister's residence and the War Ministry. Only when the Emperor Hirohito made it known that he disapproved did the coup collapse. Its ringleaders were shot, but the drift to militarism continued.

Ever since the twelfth century, Japanese society had been dominated by a feudal military ideal, with the samurai class at the top, which idealised the life of the warrior. It provided a high-class code of loyalty, honour and absolute ruthlessness. And although the feudal system had long since disappeared, this *bushido* tradition provided the whole basis for training the new military elite.

But with a power vacuum at the heart of Japanese society, even the elite suffered from irreconcilable differences – both between the military and other sections of the leadership, and within the military as well. After 1936, it became part of the constitution that the army and navy chiefs had to sit in the cabinet as War Minister and Navy Minister. Without their involvement, the decisions taken were invalid, so either could hold the government to ransom simply by threatening to resign – and as Japan plummeted to war, and civilian politicians risked assassination in their struggle for peace, this is exactly what they did.

But if the war in Europe began because

foolhardy militarists were appeased by unimaginative politicians, the war in the Pacific began the other way around – from a determination not to fuel Japan's increasingly aggressive military regime. Public opinion in the USA was furious about Japanese behaviour in China, and American diplomats were in no mood to appease Japan's hard-line leaders: their sanctions were effective and imposed rigorously. But the Americans did not fully understand the Japanese: although the architect of the attack on Pearl Harbour was regarded by the American public as brutal extremist, actually Admiral Isokuru Yamamoto was thoughtful, imaginative and very cautious.

Yamamoto was teetotal, but he was so surprised when he was appointed as commander-in-chief of the Japanese Combined Fleet in 1939 that he drank a whole pint of beer. He was also a careful strategist. He knew that an enormous US naval programme would soon tip the balance against him in the Pacific, and if Germany won the war – as it seemed on the verge of doing – it might discourage Japanese expansionism just as Britain, America and the Netherlands had done before.

To help make the decision, the group of nationalists in charge of the army forced a former prime minister back into office. This was Prince Fumimaro Konoye, a well-known hypochondriac who regularly protected himself with a germ mask in large meetings, but – when he took office in July 1940 – he was one of the few Japanese leaders who could hold the factions together. His government understood that the war in Europe provided them with a unique opportunity to get what they wanted without fighting, and he was determined to achieve this.

Then, on 27 September, the Japanese ambassador to Berlin, Saburo Kurusu, signed the pact which brought Japan into the Axis. This was intended as a defensive alliance to ward off the threat of an American declaration of war: if Roosevelt moved against one member of the Axis, he would now move against them all. "The era of democracy is finished," said the hard-line Japanese foreign minister and close friend of Konoye, Yosuke Matsuoka.

But two days after the French surrendered to the Nazis, Roosevelt responded by freezing Japanese assets in the USA and putting a full embargo on oil exports to Japan. The British and Dutch did the same, cutting Japanese oil imports by as much as 90 per cent. A nervous Japanese cabinet calculated that, unless the embargo was lifted by the spring, their economy would collapse.

Actually, there were loopholes in the embargo designed to make sure the Japanese were not forced into an impossible position, but there the carefully laid plans of Cordell Hull began to go wrong. Although the Japanese could apply for specific releases of funds to buy oil, Hull's assistant Dean Acheson turned all their applications down. Hull did not find this out until September, and by then any relaxation of the rules would look like a climbdown, so the Japanese were stuck with a total blockade.

Still desperate to avoid war, Konoye asked for a personal meeting with the US president, but Roosevelt's advisers warned him that Konoye would have too little power to enforce any agreement, so he refused to meet him. The rebuff was enough to tip Konoye from power, and he resigned on 16 October after a last minute appeal to the army to withdraw from China. If you can't decide one way or the other on war, you should resign, he was told by the nationalist war minister Hideki Tojo.

Tojo was a rare populist politician, instantly recognisable in public by his short stature and glasses, but he was also one of the most extreme hawks in the cabinet. When he became prime minister, Japanese diplomats hoped it would be a signal to Roosevelt that they were serious about their demands. Peace was to last only another seven weeks, but they were seven weeks of intense diplomatic exchanges.

When Japanese negotiators went home appalled, war seemed inevitable, but the Allies were not clear where the Japanese would strike. American and British reports were showing increasing Japanese naval activity in south east Asia. Military experts had weighed up the possibilities and decided that the hammer blow was likely to land either on the Americans in the Philippines or on the important British base of Singapore.

But the Japanese war plan, which meant overwhelming the whole of their so-called Co-prosperity Sphere as quickly as possible, did still have one important flaw: the American fleet at Pearl Harbour. Yamamoto, who was also the leading proponent of air power in the Japanese navy, came up with the solution. Inspired by the successful British attack on the Italian fleet at Taranto, he planned to use his carriers to wipe out the US fleet at anchor. On 1 December, the Japanese Imperial Council ruled that the nation's existence was at stake and they agreed to his plan.

The normally silent Hirohito spoke quietly at the end of the meeting, confirming his view that war was probably the lesser of two evils.

In fact, the Japanese fleet had already been at sea for five days. Now Yamamoto could signal his squadron with the secret code – 'Climb Mount Niitaka 1208' – which meant that there was no going back, and the attack should go ahead. On 6 December, the American code-breakers intercepted part of a long message of Japanese grievances sent to their embassy in Washington, instructing them to hand over the whole message at 1pm the following day – a Sunday.

Why would they want to deliver a message on Sunday? "This means war," said Roosevelt, when he was shown the text. But it was Saturday night, and the message was not shown to the army and navy chiefs, and anyway none of them had imagined a possible attack on Pearl Harbour. As Washington awoke the next morning, the decks of aircraft carriers of the Japanese fleet were a hive of activity ready for a dawn attack.

Indianapolis was delivering supplies and troops to Johnson Island, south west of Pearl Harbour, when the news came through of the Japanese attack on 7 December, the day which Roosevelt would say later would "live in infamy". The peacetime furniture, including the chairs and wardrobes from Roosevelt's stateroom, was thrown overboard because it was inflammable, and *Indianapolis* steamed to intercept the Japanese carrier fleet which had carried out the attack. Perhaps it was just as well, at the time, that it failed to find them. Without proper air support, *Indianapolis* would probably have succumbed in the way that the British fleet in Singapore had done on three days later.

The crew did not see action for nearly three months. But *Indianapolis* was in the south Pacific on 20 February 1942 when they were attacked by twin-engined bombers, as the Japanese were organising their forces to take Port Moresby in New Guinea.

In the following months, the crew shifted their area of operation to the North Pacific as part of the campaign around Midway Island, after the Japanese had taken Attu and Kiska islands, where *Indianapolis* was part of the US forces which finally managed to penetrate the thick fog around the islands to bombard Kiska and the shipping in the harbour.

It was also a critical period of disappointment

for the Japanese submarine fleet, forced to operate in freezing conditions, in huge submarines which had been designed for the tropics, and in tasks supporting the beleaguered garrison. Among those involved was a torpedo officer called Mochitsura Hashimoto, whose destiny was to be bound up intimately with the fate of the *Indianapolis*.

Among the American stars in the battle of Midway, credited with turning the tide in the Pacific, was a cruiser commander called Raymond Spruance. It was Spruance who took command of the American fleet when Halsey became too ill with eczema to continue at that critical moment. It was a controversial appointment, and Halsey's advice – Spruance had no experience operating with carriers – but it proved an inspired one. Spruance's calm deliberation led to the sinking of four Japanese carriers for the loss of one and, in one fell swoop, turned the tide in the Pacific.

Shortly after the battle, Spruance became chief of staff to Admiral Chester Nimitz, the Pacific Fleet's commander-in-chief, and from there it was a short series of increasingly prominent appointments before Spruance was put in charge of the Central Pacific Force. Nimitz was testing an unusual arrangement. His Third Fleet and his Fifth Fleet were actually the same ships, but the two admirals – Spruance and Bill Halsey – alternated in command, together with their respective staff. When Halsey was running the fleet, Spruance and his staff were at Pearl Harbour, planning the next operations, and vice versa. It was not just an unusual arrangement; it also confused Japanese intelligence. "We changed drivers and kept the horses," said Halsey later.

Just as the Japanese were paralysed by inter-service rivalries, Nimitz and MacArthur fought out an undeclared feud and had to hold the rival army and marine commanders apart at critical moments. Luckily Halsey and Spruance liked each other and got on well, despite their great differences in temperament. While Halsey was a risk-taker, Spruance was careful: Spruance was Mr Spock to Halsey's Captain Kirk, according to Spruance's biographer Thomas Buell. It was said that many senior officers preferred to serve under Spruance because of his careful planning, though the press loved Halsey and so did the ordinary sailors.

Spruance put himself and his small staff aboard *Indianapolis* and, for most of the rest of the war, this was his flagship and his home at sea, through the campaigns that captured the Marianas, through to Iwo Jima and Okinawa. He liked classical music, never smoked and hardly ever drank. He made himself a cup of cocoa every morning and made light of his reputation as a tactician, never discussing his feelings or opinions in public. "Some people believe that when I am quiet that I am thinking some deep and important thoughts," he wrote later, "when the fact is that I am thinking of nothing at all. My mind is blank."

Spruance was the great fighting admiral of the American navy, who never quite received the recognition he deserved – or entered the nation's consciousness in the way that Nimitz or Halsey did. He was also a great walker, dealing with the weight of the stress of command by walking for several miles every day, usually around *Indianapolis'* quarter deck (now steel not teak), usually eating raw onions and often with his shirt off. On one occasion during the battle for Iwo Jima, he was asked to get below, so that the anti-aircraft guns could open fire. He was quiet, reserved and insisted on light lunches of salad and soup for his staff, much to their frustration.

The war in the Pacific was an overwhelmingly aerial one at sea, fought by fleets not usually within sight of each other. The damage that could be done by planes on a naval force was devastating, as the destruction of the British Force Z was to find out to its cost, without air cover, just days after the Pearl Harbour raid. Part of the story of the *Indianapolis* is the way that the US navy, unlike the Japanese navy – and in some ways unlike the British – was able to break through the inbuilt conservatism of military hierarchies to learn the lessons that needed to be learned. The British failed to learn the lessons of their own aerial success against the Italian fleet in 1940. The Americans realised how much naval warfare had changed. The Japanese military faced real problems from the in-fighting between the navy and the army – the army even built their own submarines, without the benefit of the navy's experience, but even their own naval submarines were not used as intended.

One man who was at the heart of the tensions within the Japanese submarine service was Mochitsura Hashimoto. At the outbreak of war in the Pacific, he was 32, having graduated from the naval academy ten years before. In December 1941, he was torpedo officer of the submarine I-24, which – together with four similar submarines –

was stationed off Pearl Harbour, waiting for their orders to attack.

There were strange structures on the deck, and had been since they left their home port at Kure, designed to secure midget submarines. The plan was to release these, and that they would then make their way into the base and attack the carriers and battleships. The plans were complex and untested, and Yamamoto – the commander-in-chief – was insisting that there should be plans in place for the recovery of the midgets after their attack: this was not to be a suicide mission. Hashimoto had seen action before, on gunboats in the Yangtze River battles, but he was as nervous as the rest of the crew. The squadron had been late sailing so had to make directly for Pearl Harbour, despite the security risk of doing so.

The day before the attack, the crew had been told that the carriers were not there, but there were eight battleships in port. This was something of a disappointment: without destroying the US carrier fleet, the attack might as well have not taken place. But it was too late to stop now. The midget submarines, aware that they would almost certainly not return, were launched. The one from I-24 had a faulty gyro compass and kept running aground, and it was captured later and its pilot imprisoned. One attacked the battleship *Arizona*. The rest of the midget submarines were either sunk, abandoned or never seen again.

It was the start of the continuing story of disappointment amongst the Japanese submarine service, which failed to live up to the high expectations placed upon it. This was partly because the tactics assigned to their submarines by the Japanese navy were flawed, and partly because – as an embattled outpost of a highly centralised and authoritarian regime – those flaws were obvious but never acted upon.

The Japanese navy had been designed for over a decade on the assumption that a war with the USA was inevitable, and the plan was always to take the initiative by destroying the American battlefleet at sea by using submarines. This was not effective. Quite the reverse: as their huge submarines failed to make an impact on the enemy fleet – which is what they were designed for – they were not assigned instead to take on the American merchant fleet, which is how the American submarines were being used with such success. In fact, all too often, they were engaged in blockade running operations to keep the besieged island garrisons supplied during the Pacific war.

Worse, the Japanese navy carried out a number

of pre-war exercises which demonstrated clearly that this was not going to be effective, at least on a systematic basis, because the submarines were simply not fast enough to maintain an attacking position on a fleet at sea when they were on the surface, and certainly not submerged. Nor did they grasp that the same would apply to the Americans, and that these were likely to use their submarines effectively in other ways.

As war loomed, with Hashimoto a committed officer in the submarine fleet, they would have only 64 submarines ready. Where they did have an important advantage was in their torpedo design. They had been tested effectively, using pure oxygen, and were highly reliable, unlike their American equivalent. In the years to come, Hashimoto would find himself fighting his own naval establishment over the equipment they were using which he believed was putting them at a disadvantage in the war at sea.

Another officer who would find himself at odds with his own naval establishment was Charles Butler McVay. McVay was extremely well-connected. His grandfather had been president of the Pittsburg Trust Company. His father, Admiral Charles McVay, had commanded the US Asiatic Fleet after the First World War, when the

Japanese and Americans had been allies. At the outbreak of war, there was no reason for thinking that he would not end his career a highly-respected and decorated admiral.

McVay had graduated from the Annapolis naval academy in 1920 and was fluent in French. He in command of a small former Yangtze gunboat, the USS *Luzon,* in 1939, a job he combined with membership of the staff of the US High Commissioner in the Philippines. From there, at the end of 1940, he took command of a naval oiler, the *Kaweah,* operating up and down the American east coast from Iceland down to the Caribbean. This meant dodging U-boats as the US navy drifted into war with Nazi Germany.

He was destined to serve with distinction on twelve different ships during the Pacific war, and to win the Silver Star for his courage under fire as second-in-command of the cruiser *Cleveland* during the battle of the Solomon Islands. The navy was his life and he rose rapidly. That is, until his encounter with Hashimoto in the final weeks of the Second World War.

Chapter 2
A final year

"The things that I remember best are the times when we had considerable differences of opinion about what we should do. These were generally resolved satisfactorily, and there is no point in rehearsing them. I think the fact that we could have differences in our ideas, and could argue and debate our various points of view up and down the line is the important thing to remember. Time for preparing our plans was short, and they had to proceed more or less simultaneously on all echelons to get things done. If orders had been handed down the line from on high, and no one had been allowed to question them or any part of them, things might, at times, have gone differently."
Admiral Raymond Spruance

In February 1944, Spruance was in *Indianapolis* while he directed Operation Hailstone against the Japanese naval base at Truk in Micronesia. Having disposed of twelve warships and thirty-two merchant vessels, Spruance led a battle group to chase the ships that were escaping. Where Spruance had critics, it was for his caution – careful not to chase the retreating Japanese fleet after Midway when he did not have adequate intelligence. On this occasion, he was bold. In fact, it was said afterwards that he had been the first four star admiral to be on board one of his own ships during the action.

Spruance watched the invasion of the Marshall Islands from the deck of *Indianapolis*, a crucial but exhausting campaign. The assault went better than his previous action, the attack on Tarawa Atoll in the Gilbert Islands where they underestimated Japanese defences. Every island captured in this period of the Pacific war became a base to organise a landing on the next one. But the crucial moment in the war came at the battle of the Philippine Sea, from 19 to 20 June 1944. It was then that Task Force 58, under Spruance in *Indianapolis,* leading a fleet of no less than fifteen aircraft carriers that massively outgunned their opponents in a battle which became known as the Great Marianas Turkey Shoot.

This was the first time since Midway that the Japanese fleet had been committed into action, and Spruance decided to delay the invasion of Guam and to move the invasion armada out of harm's way until the battle was over. On the first day, no fewer than 346 Japanese planes were shot down. As the campaign developed, *Indianapolis* was involved in speeding Spruance backwards and forwards to conferences of senior commanders and then back to the action. Not for nothing had Spruance chosen a cruiser. Then, on 29 July, she became the first American warship to enter Apra Harbour on Guam since the start of the war. *Indianapolis* was cramped and swelteringly hot – the fans interfered with the radar so they were turned off – but Spruance spent only a brief period with his flag in the battleship *New Jersey* before he came back to the speed and flexibility of his cruiser flagship.

The battle of the Philippine Sea provided Spruance with his greatest maritime success, sinking three carriers and destroying more than 600 planes. The defeat was on such a scale that, when Halsey led American forces at the battle of Leyte Gulf later in the year, he found that the remaining Japanese carriers were being used mainly as decoys, without either planes or the aircrews to fly them. Once again, Spruance faced criticisms for defending his invasion fleet rather than going after the remaining Japanese carriers, but he felt that he could not afford to gamble.

It was after the Philippine Sea that the Japanese fell back on suicide squadrons, using the title *kamikaze* – the name for the divine wind which had saved Japan from a Mongol fleet in 1281. The kamikaze planes are well-known, and still provide a frisson of horror, especially now that suicide bombs are more common. Less known were the suicide speedboats and the *kaiten*, the manned torpedoes which were carried by the larger submarines towards the end of the war, carrying their pilots at speed to a certain death, either in an explosion or by drowning when the fuel ran out.

The attitude of the submarine officers towards the *kaiten* pilots they carried with them was of a kind of sad respect – respect for their courage and sad that their lives were going to be sacrificed. Among those carrying them was Hashimoto.

Mochitsura Hashimoto had begun 1942 with a bombardment of Midway Island before the battle. One of the purposes of the Japanese submarines was bombardment – it explained their enormous size and the calibre of their guns. But once again, they were disappointing in action. The submarine crews had mistaken the flashes of returning fire for hits. Six months later, he was graduating from an advanced course for potential submarine commanders and – in June 1942 – he was in command of the small submarine R-31 in the Yokosura command, wrestling with the issue of how to supply their garrison on Guadalcanal.

Once again, this was not what the submarine fleet had been designed to do but there was no questioning the high command. Was it possible to shoot bags of rice out through torpedo tubes? Hashimoto was charged with experimenting with putting it in biscuit tins in Tokyo Bay.

There was a submarine fleet meeting of commanding officers which resisted plans to resupply the army in this way. It meant almost certain death and it wasn't what the submarines had been designed for. But the imperial command said that the garrison must be supplied at all costs, and consequently their submarines were recalled from around the Indian Ocean, where they had been beginning to play havoc with British and allied shipping.

Early the following year, Hashimoto was in command of a much bigger submarine, I-158, this time carrying out experiments with radar. Radar was a problem for Japanese submarines, the victim of the usual inter- and intra-service in-fighting that beset the Japanese war effort. Radar had only been developed as early as the mid-1930s and played a significant role in the Battle of Britain in 1940. By this stage in the war, most US ships carried some kind of radar, and so did most of their submarines. But the Japanese submarine fleet was still struggling to develop an effective model. Submarine commanders blamed their lack of radar for the propensity of their huge vessels to run aground, and their relative vulnerability to air attack.

"It was, in fact a fight between the blind and those who could see," wrote Hashimoto later. "The enemy was able to track us down even through the fog and open fire without warning. Many boats were sacrificed needlessly." Part of the problem was that American pilots were aware of the difference: American submarines would have seen them coming and dived; if a submarine was caught on the surface, there wasn't any doubt – it was Japanese.

The naval authorities were extraordinarily complacent about the problem. Submarines without radar were just plain suicide wrote the captain of the I-174. But the admiral in command of submarines replied that "even though boats failed to return, they were playing their part just the same." So when Hashimoto saw an aircraft radar set in use at the Kure naval station, he asked to borrow it.

With the support of the senior officer of the 11th Submarine Squadron, he installed it in I-158 and tested it out at sea over three days and found that it worked. The results were sent by urgent signal to Tokyo. The reply was to question why he had the temerity to carry out trials without the approval of the naval technical department.

When he was finally given permission to go to Tokyo to see the technical department himself, he was assured that the naval version was nearly ready – which he knew was not the case. Instead he went to see the Technical Research Bureau, where officials gave him a more enthusiastic reaction. This in turn enraged the naval technical department. Instead of giving him the go-ahead for taking the aircraft version of radar to sea, he was given approval to buy an extra pair of binoculars. "It was indeed regrettable that our headquarters staff were more concerned with preserving their dignity than giving proper appreciation to active service conditions," he wrote.

For the time being, the only radar fitted on Japanese submarines was the set donated by the

German U-boat command when one of them took the rare and risky voyage for a well-earned refit at the U-boat base in Brest (German naval engineers assessed the Japanese designs and found their hulls vibrated too much to be silent)..

In January 1944, Hashimoto set sail for the Eastern Solomons, in command of Ro-44. He arrived in Truk to find their submarine depot ship sunk at its moorings. Unusually, the four submarines sent on this mission all came home safely. "True, they hadn't all carried out their allotted tasks, but it was a long time since all boats had returned safely form an operation," he wrote later. "Some four months later, by the end of the battle of Saipan in June 1944, the other three captains had all been killed in action and I was the only one left."

Back in Kure, waiting for his new command – the state-of the-art submarine monster, I-58 – to be fitted out, he returned to his personal battle, struggling to resist an order to remove his aircraft radar from the submarines. He came to the conclusion that the radar approved equipment was not working as well as it should because no skilled electricians had been drafted. He managed to persuade the personnel department to send him two, only to find that the dockyard was refusing to fit the equipment he wanted.

As Hashimoto was fighting the battle of the submarine radar, Charles McVay was working on shore in Washington in the highly prestigious position of chairman of the Joint Intelligence Staff, working in the office of the vice-chief of naval operations, and working with the Combined Chiefs of Staff. It was the highest intelligence unit, working directly with British opposite numbers in London. It was an important job but McVay wanted to go back to sea. In November 1944, he got his wish and was appointed in command of *Indianapolis*. It was another glittering position, to be what the British called 'flag captain' to Spruance. It was also his first command.

In the meantime, the next planned island hop on the way to Japan was Iwo Jima, only four miles long and 660 miles from Tokyo, and the Americans needed this heavily defended island to help provide escort planes for their bombers. The planning of its capture had begun as early as September 1943, with the commander of the US marines in the Pacific 'Howling Mad' Smith in command.

For 72 devastating days at the end of 1944, the

US navy and air force pulverised the defences of the island in the longest and heaviest bombardment of the Pacific war. As many as 450 invasion ships arrived offshore on 19 February 1945, and 45 minutes after that the first landing craft set off for the 4,000 yard dash to shore, and the first of seven marine battalions was soon ashore.

When they were no more than 300 yards inland, they realised that the Japanese defenders had been prepared for them. The next three days saw the bitterest fighting the US marines had ever faced. It took three days to struggle up to the peak of Suribacki on the tip of the island and raise the flag in the famous photograph, recreated after the war as a memorial outside Arlington Cemetery in Virginia.

By 9 March, the marines had reached the other end of the island and the mopping-up operation could begin, hampered by suicidal charges from the remaining Japanese troops. But the battle was far from over yet. The remains of the island had been turned into a vast network of fortified tunnels, manned by troops who had sworn to kill at least ten American soldiers before they were themselves killed. "Have not eaten or drunk for five days," wrote the Japanese commander,

General Tadamichi Kuribayashi on 15 March. "But fighting spirit is running high. We are going to fight bravely to the last moment."

They did just that. Only 1,083 of the 23,000 Japanese troops defending the island were ever taken prisoner, while nearly 7,000 US marines had been killed, winning 24 Medals of Honour in the process. Before the fighting had ended, the first US bombers had landed on the island. On 7 April, the first escorting Mustangs took off from the island to accompany a daylight air raid on Tokyo. Three months after the battle, as many as 850 US bombers had made emergency landings on Iwo Jima. Without the battle to secure it, nearly all would have crashed into the Pacific. But the ferocity of the Iwo Jima battle scared the US chiefs of staff: if the battle for a tiny island near Japan would take that amount of effort – what would it mean to invade Japan itself?

Throughout the battle for Iwo Jima, *Indianapolis* had taken part in the bombardment. At one stage, Spruance took his walk along the open deck, oblivious of the fact that the main armament was bombarding the island defences on the other side.

Okinawa, the next island, was 67 miles long and its invasion took three months and left 12,500 American dead. The Japanese imperial command had held back at least 2,000 planes in reserve for the occasion and American planners realised it could be the toughest battle yet.

The invasion was designated Operation Iceberg, and the task was given to the 170,000 troops of the US Tenth Army under General Simon Buckner, and it began after another massive bombardment from air and sea which started on 25 March. For the first time, the Americans were joined in the Pacific by the British fleet, where the steel decks of the British carriers were tested to the limit by the kamikaze attacks which had damaged three US fast carriers. Both the British and Americans had to develop techniques to deal with the kamikazes, posting anti-aircraft ships at a distance from the carriers and battleships to knock them out before they could get close to their targets. But they still succeeded in causing enormous damage: nearly 5,000 US naval personnel were killed by them during the Okinawa landings.

These began on 1 April and the whole operation soon developed as a re-run as Iwo Jima. Just as they had there, the invaders crawled ashore with little opposition, but then came up against entrenched Japanese positions further into the island. From 6 April, the Japanese air attacks began in earnest, with nearly 700 planes – half of which were kamikazes – sent to Okinawa: as many as 1,900 kamikaze missions were flown during the operation. Even the Japanese flagship *Yamato* was sent out on a kamikaze mission of its own, with a small escort and only enough fuel for the outward journey. It was finally sunk after a two-hour attack from US planes on 7 April, without ever having fired its enormous main armament against an enemy battleship.

On Okinawa itself, there were heavy casualties among the Americans: on average it was only three weeks there before they were wounded. Those killed included Buckner, who was killed by an anti-tank shell on 18 June. Almost all those captured were killed shortly afterwards by the Japanese.

On 3 May, the Japanese defenders launched a suicidal counter-attack, and for the next seven weeks, Americans losses mounted in a series of confused and bitter battles, often fighting hand to hand and using flame-throwers to flush out resistance from the islands caves. Japanese losses were enormous: nearly 110,000 died, only 7,400 surrendered and many of the Japanese civilians on the island jumped to their deaths from the steep cliffs on the island rather than become prisoners. Another 75,000 local civilians had been killed in the ferocious battles, including 85 Japanese student nurses who were killed accidentally after hiding in a cavern, still celebrated by the Japanese as the 'Cave of the Virgins'.

When they finally attacked the Japanese base at Naha, it took ten days to fight their way into the headquarters cave, where they found that 200 wounded soldiers and senior officers had killed themselves, including the base commander. The leaders of the Japanese forces on Okinawa, generals Ushijima and Sho, killed themselves on 22 June. "I depart without regret, shame or obligations," said Sho in his final message.

It was during the invasion of Okinawa that the luck of *Indianapolis* finally began to run out. The previous week had seen her bombarding the Japanese defences, but 31 March was the day when the string of events began that were to lead to her disappearance in the middle of the Pacific. She was operating as a flagship with Spruance aboard, as usual, when she was hit by a bomb dropped by a kamikaze pilot. The bomb went straight through the ship, through the mess room table, where sailors were having lunch, and burst against the hull. The plane itself crashed onto the deck but failed to explode and had to be rocked overboard – a delicate operation since the payload of explosives might have gone up any time.

Nine crewmen were killed and, although the flooding was contained quickly, *Indianapolis* had been seriously damaged and slowed. Spruance left immediately to transfer his flag to the battleship *New Mexico*.

Oil began the war and it was the shortage of oil which was now strangling the Japanese war effort and bringing the war to a close. The oil from the captured Dutch East Indies was coming out of the ground, but the blockade by Allied submarines was increasingly stopping it from reaching Japan. Only five per cent got there in 1944, and none at all in 1945. So much of the Japanese merchant fleet had been sunk by the beginning of 1945 that American submarines were being diverted to pick up the crews of ditched aircrews.

The activities of the Allied submarines were kept secret by the US navy throughout the war, but by the beginning of 1945, Task Force 71 consisted of 75 submarines – 40 American, 30 British and five Dutch. And having driven nearly all the Japanese fleet out of the Indian Ocean, British midget submarines were being sent to attack Japanese cruisers in Singapore harbour.

Since the fall of Okinawa, the Japanese knew they could not win the war. Worse, the US air force was dropping 40,000 tons of bombs on the Japanese mainland every month. As much as 90 per cent of their navy and merchant fleet had been sunk, and in 60 cities and large towns, nearly half the buildings had been bombed flat. Shortage of air fuel meant that the air force could provide almost no resistance against the continuous raids.

Without enough fuel to run their fleet or train their pilots, the Japanese imperial command could do little more than watch the destruction by Allied ships and planes. They were also now afraid of internal collapse: the thought police were afraid that growing disaffection and defeatism would bring a communist takeover if the war was lost. Over 700 anonymous letter-writers were prosecuted during the war, by 1944 Tokyo police investigating 15 to 20 new 'rumours' a day. The emperor Hirohito was being sent a stream of angry cards: one postcard from a twelve-year-old boy said simply: 'Stupid emperor'. In February 1945, former prime minister Fumimaro urged Hirohito to surrender quickly and save the country from revolution.

The Allied military planners who had made such a success of D-Day were carefully developing plans for the invasion of the Japanese mainland, and MacArthur was estimating another million casualties before Japan would surrender, an event he predicted for the winter of 1946. But the next stage in the approach to Japan, the invasion of Kyushu planned for November 1945, never happened.

On 5 April, after the news that the Americans had landed on Okinawa, the elderly Admiral Kantaro Suzuki became prime minister. He was already 78 – a war hero from the war with Russia forty years before, and enough of a dove to have narrowly escaped with his life during the 1936 coup – and although convinced of the need for peace, he needed more energy than he had for the delicate balance he needed. If he talked of peace too openly, he risked a military coup, but unless he did so, the destruction would continue.

So he re-appointed as foreign minister Shigenori Togo, who had been living in retirement since the failure of his efforts to avoid war in 1941. Togo only agreed to accept the position on condition that his only job was to find peace.

In those circumstances, it was nothing short of miraculous that Hashimoto was still alive to receive orders in the summer of 1945, and to take I-58 to sea. He had been in dock, in charge of equipping his new command, and – in this bitter phase – the war had also been passing him by. To his immense frustration, he had not sunk a single ship. He prayed regularly at the Shinto shrine they carried on board. He had an unconfirmed hit on a tanker off Guam and had been under constant attack during the Okinawa operation, but it was partly because he had managed to stay so inconspicuous so successfully that he had survived at all. In fact, by July 1945, I-58 was one of only four Japanese ocean-going submarines still in operation.

I-58 was enormous, over 350 foot long and with a crew of a hundred, including a number of *kaiten*, the human manned suicide torpedoes. It was equipped with a deck gun and an anti-aircraft gun and a hanger with a seaplane, and it was driven by twin diesel engines which could propel it at 17 knots on the surface. This was a state-of-the-art submarine in so many ways, except that it had not benefited from some of the technical advances in the British, German and American submarines. But it had the benefit of some peculiar defensive innovations: it was covered in a rubber coating to avoid the sonar pings that would bounce off a metal hull.

I-58 finished the process of fitting out only in March 1945, while *Indianapolis* was still acting as a flagship off Okinawa. Then there were trails and shake-down cruises. Before Hashimoto set sail from Kure on 16 July, he was given orders to attack enemy shipping off the Philippines. He was going back to the war with relief and with the added responsibility of carrying six *kaiten* and their pilots, aware that on his orders six men would sail to their deaths.

But he was equally aware of their motivations: most of his officer colleagues in Japanese submarines were now dead. By setting sail in I-58, he knew he was very unlikely to survive. What the *kaiten* pilots were doing, in their disarming enthusiasm, waving their ornamental swords, was to take back control and choose the place and time of their own sacrifice. "It was very sad to think he was billed for certain death in this attempt to turn the tide of war," wrote Hashimoto about a kaiten colleague:

"Painful though it was to think of sending these men on such expeditions, the times were such that the number of those who did not return were growing apace in fields quite outside special units, and both old and young alike were departing from this world. In such a situation, sooner or later, their fate was inevitable."

Chapter 3
A disappearance

"The only way I could tell they were dead was to put my finger in their eye. If they pupils were dilated and they didn't blink, I assumed they were dead."
Dr Lewis Haynes, survivor

On Sunday 15 July, still on Mare Island but aware that repairs to *Indianapolis* had been suddenly speeded up, McVay was called to a top level briefing. He was told that the ship must be ready by the following day, and that he must sail to San Francisco and take on board what was described as a secret project. It was explained that the cruiser *Pensacola* had been earmarked for the mission but had developed an engine fault during her sea trials. *Indianapolis* had weeks still to go until her repairs had been completed, but no other cruiser was available.

In the next few hours, McVay oversaw the loading of 60,000 tons of fuel, plus stores and ammunition. He was also uncomfortably aware that a quarter of his crew were straight from basic training and it would be necessary – as soon as they had disposed of the secret project – to do some intensive training on board.

As Hashimoto set sail from Kure, by coincidence, McVay was taking *Indianapolis* to sea from Mare Island down the coast of California to San Francisco. There remains some dispute among eyewitnesses whether it was one or two heavy black canisters that were winched aboard at the wharf there, accompanied by a radiologist, disguised as an artillery captain. The black canister (assuming there was, as seems likely, only one) was taken to the flag lieutenant's cabin and welded to the floor. The flag lieutenant was a member of Spruance's staff so he wasn't there.

Casting off again from San Francisco shortly afterwards, there was an unnerving send off from families of the crew as she slipped under the Golden Gate. Somebody had defied orders that their sailing should remain completely quiet. Once at sea, McVay was told that his ship was now under the orders of the Commander-in-Chief and must not be diverted from its mission for any reason whatever. The existence of the black canister was now common knowledge among the crew but they did not know what it was. McVay had been chairman of a key intelligence committee, so he was better equipped than anyone to guess – but he believed it contained components for some kind of biological weapon. The Commander-in-Chief was after all the president, now Harry Truman. McVay told the crew that, if the ship was to sink, the canister had to be but put on its own raft and set adrift, before anyone could think of saving themselves.

Nazi Germany had surrendered in May but the war in the Pacific carried on, each new twist more terrifying than the last. We know now that the Second World War had only weeks to run – and partly because of the black canister that *Indianapolis* now carried – but at the time, most of the navy believed there were months, if not years, of fighting still to come. The invasion of Japan loomed ahead..

There was music from a naval band as I-58 left Kure the same day, then it was a short journey to the *kaiten* base and a series of ceremonies to celebrate their bravery. Next day, it was back to base because the periscopes of the kaiten turned out to be defective. Then it was fast, on the surface at night and submerged during the day, to the Okinawa-Guam convoy route. The moon was waning and Hashimoto was impatient to get in position when there would be enough moonlight to be effective. He still prayed for success every evening at the ship's shrine.

McVay's orders had told him to proceed fast to Tinian Island, five miles south west of Saipan. Inside his black canister, though he did not know it, were the heaviest components of the atomic bomb that was known as Little Boy and about half the uranium-235 in the USA, which had come in convoy directly from the Los Alamos Laboratory in New Mexico.

Though neither Hashimoto nor McVay knew it, both sides were now desperate to find a way to avoid an invasion of mainland Japan. Prime Minister Suzuki's mistake – against Togo's advice – was to put out peace feelers via Stalin, in the hope that he would be an intermediary, but Stalin was now committed to fighting in the Far East himself, and he rejected the idea. By intercepting Suzuki's messages to his ambassador in Moscow, the Allies knew there was a good chance that dropping their insistence on unconditional surrender might well persuade the emperor to overrule his cabinet.

In fact the Japanese cabinet stayed divided even after 20 June, when Hirohito had summoned the Supreme War Direction Council and told them: "You will consider the question of ending the war as soon as possible." Three were in favour of immediate unconditional surrender, but the army minister and chiefs of staff still wanted some conditions attached.

As Hashimoto and McVay were setting sail, the Allied leaders were meeting outside Berlin at the Potsdam conference, where trust in Stalin had been replaced by growing suspicion among the western negotiators. American chiefs of staff were increasingly nervous about Stalin's promised entry into the Pacific war, and the Allies were now regretting the promise they had forced out of him: the last thing they now wanted was Soviet interference in the Far East.

But there was now another consideration. The first atomic bomb which the USA and Britain had been struggling to develop was nearly ready for testing, even as *Indianapolis* was carrying the components for the second. Churchill and Truman, were planning to tell Stalin about this as soon as they knew the result of the crucial first nuclear test, and maybe – they thought – it might be sensible to wait for the showdown with the Soviets until after they knew they had a unique weapon of mass destruction safely in their hands.

On 15 July, the day that McVay had been ordered to sail, Truman had arrived at the conference with Stalin and Churchill to receive a cryptic message. "Operated on this morning," it said. "Diagnosis not yet complete, but results seem satisfactory, and already exceed expectations". Churchill received a similarly coded note which said "babes satisfactorily born", which he didn't understand. The world's first nuclear test in the New Mexico desert had been a success: British agreement to use the bomb if necessary had already been given back in 1943, so it was now up to Truman. And although they did tell Stalin about the new weapon, in retrospect neither leader believed he had quite taken it in. Some kind of demonstration seemed necessary.

During the conference, Churchill went back to Britain for the results of the general election and found that he had lost. He was replaced at Potsdam by his own former deputy, Clement Attlee, and the conference ended by issuing a stern warning to the Japanese government, urging them to surrender or face complete destruction. The bomb was not mentioned.

There then followed Suzuki's second mistake. His reply included the ambiguous Japanese phrase that he would 'withhold comment on' the warning, but this was translated for Truman as meaning 'ignore'. In fact, foreign minister Togo was sending an urgent message to his Moscow ambassador: "Since the loss of one day relative to this present matter may result in a thousand years of regret, it is requested that you immediately have a talk with Molotov". But Viachislav Molotov, Stalin's foreign minister, could not be trusted. He would delay the conversation until 8 August, by which time it was exactly three months since VE Day and Stalin had declared war on Japan.

Indianapolis reached Tinian Island on 26 July. It was a small spot in the middle of the Pacific, just ten miles long, but capable of providing a runway for the huge B-29 Superfortresses, with wingspans stretch for 140 feet, that were now bombarding the mainland of Japan. It was now the largest airbase in the world. McVay had sped there through heavy seas at a gruelling speed of 28 knots.

By that time, Hashimoto was taking I-58 onto the 'Peddie' convoy route between Guam and Leyte. The truth was that, since the action had moved from Okinawa to planning an invasion of the Japanese mainland, this was a backwater of the war. His hope was based on the possibility that the merchant and warships he encountered there would hardly be expecting a submarine attack – as indeed they did not.

There was no end-of-term feeling about Guam and Leyte, as we might now expect, because the war was expected to carry on. But the conversations were not about the dangers of the waters between the two. They were about how best to end the war with a minimum of casualties. As senior officers knew, there were in fact six rival allied teams in Washington working on different plans to stage the inevitable invasion. As they did not know, there was also a seventh option: dropping the highly secret nuclear bomb. It may be that the latest feud between Admiral Nimitz and General Macarthur in the Philippines was the main subject of conversation, over whether the Seventh Fleet, where Macarthur was temporarily in command, should actually be merged permanently with his army.

McVay was at Tinian for only six hours, enough to unload the black canister, and to be given further orders. He was told to go to Guam, 120 miles to the south, and then on to Leyte where he was to report to Admiral Jesse Oldendorf and receive orders as part of Task Force 95, which was due for a series of exercises. As it turned out, a signal warning that *Indianapolis* was on the way to Leyte had arrived there but had not been decoded because of a muddle about who it was intended for. Crucially, the signal included no date for an anticipated arrival. If there had been, there might have been more reason for some of the naval personnel to notice that she was missing.

It was less than a day's journey to Guam and McVay left the ship immediately to see the senior naval officer on the island. Was there an escort available to Leyte, McVay asked? There was not – most of the available destroyers were being concentrated ready for the invasion. The risk from enemy submarines in the area was minimal, he was told. He was given orders to zigzag as a precaution during daylight hours, and at his own discretion at night. These orders were to prove the lynchpin at his court martial five months later.

What McVay was not told, though presumably the authorities in Guam did not know either, was that there was actually some reason to be nervous of submarines on the route to Leyte after all. A periscope had been seen there and reported and crucially, a destroyer had been sunk nearby only a week before, and the American code breakers had intercepted Hashimoto's orders as he left Kure. They knew where he was heading. But, unlike the

British, the Americans had no systematic way of using that information: it was often considered too sensitive to use at all. So McVay was given no extra reason for caution on his trip to Leyte. Nor was he given an escort. He was not concerned about that: *Indianapolis* had made many unaccompanied voyages, speeding alone across the Pacific at such a rate that most submarines would not be able to get a shot at her – unless, of course, they happened to be in the perfect position.

Hashimoto had spent ten days on other convoy routes but had seen absolutely nothing. On 27 July, he arrived in I-58 on the Guam-Leyte route, just as McVay was having lunch with Spruance on Guam. Early the next morning, he sighted a tanker, being escorted by a destroyer. The tanker turned away at a critical moment in his attack: he fired two of his *kaiten*, and heard two explosions, but could see nothing through the periscope.

At 7.30pm on 29 July, the darkness was falling and the moon and stars were covered by cloud. It was pitch black and McVay ordered that *Indianapolis* should stop zigzagging, which his orders allowed him to at his own discretion when the visibility was poor. McVay had set the speed at just over 15 knots, so that they could arrive at Leyte in time for anti-aircraft practice before the scheduled manoeuvres. It was swelteringly hot and, as it grew darker, the crew began to bed down for the night on the open deck. McVay and Hashimoto did not know it, but they were heading straight towards each other.

At around 11pm, the hydroplanes officer on I-58 reported to Hashimoto that he could hear a tinkling sound. It is usually believed that he could hear the sound of clinking dishes in the galley in *Indianapolis*, a testament to the extraordinary way that sound can travel through water. Hashimoto went up onto the conning tower and could see that, suddenly, the night was beginning to clear. The moon was now visible and the horizon was beginning to become sharper. Back down in the control room, he heard the shout from the navigator, Lieutenant Hiromu Tanaka, on the conning tower that there was a ship. He raced up the ladder and turned his binoculars in the direction he had been pointed, "Without doubt there was a black spot which was clearly visible on the horizon on the rays of the moon," wrote Hashimoto later. He gave the order to dive.

Up went the periscope again. It would be almost impossible to spot a periscope at night, and the conditions of visibility were all in his favour. The ship that was approaching was etched out in moonlight, when his periscope would be part of the gloom. But one thing worried him: why was this ship making straight for him? Was it a destroyer using some kind of radar which had identified him as an enemy submarine? Was he about to come under attack?

The time passed. At a distance of about 4,000 yards, it became clear that this ship was much bigger than a destroyer. It was also clear that it was alone. The *kaiten* pilots were nagging him to let them launch: if this was a big ship, or even a battleship, they wanted the honour of sacrificing their lives to sink it. But Hashimoto did not want to be responsible for their deaths if he could sink the ship in the conventional way. The trouble was that he needed to make calculations about its speed and, without knowing what kind of ship it was – without some kind of profile that could identify it – it was very hard to estimate its speed.

He waited for it to change direction or zigzag so that he could see it and get a better broadside view. It didn't. But judging by the large superstructure on the foredeck, he decided it was probably a battleship of the Idaho class. That must have made him under-estimate the speed; Idaho class battleships had a top speed of only 20 knots, which it had not achieved for many years. If the target had been zigzagging, it would have been an easier shot. As it was, the submarine was in a position to fire at midnight, and a few minutes into 30 July, Hashimoto fired six torpedoes in a spread pattern just ahead of its path. The target was only a mile away. It would take only a minute or so for the torpedoes to hit or miss. He stood down the *kaiten* pilots.

Donald Blum was one of the officers on watch that night on the bridge of *Indianapolis,* driving through the Pacific at 17 knots, now visible in the moonlight. The first he, or anyone else aboard, knew of the attack was when a huge explosion in the bows rocked the ship, tearing off the front of the ship. A moment or so later, there was another huge explosion amidships, which hit the powder magazine for the ship's main armament. "At first I thought it was a boiler exploding," he wrote later. There was chaos and screaming on board as the injured and uninjured struggled to work out what had happened.

Even with no bows, *Indianapolis* was still ploughing through the water, and the bridge was unable to contact the engine room. Within minutes the ship was beginning to list over the starboard as the speed dropped. Fires were raging in the middle of the ship. Below the bridge, McVay had been blown out of bed by the force of the explosion, and made his way quickly, still naked, to find out what had happened. It was difficult to grasp the extent of the damage, though it was pretty clear that they must have been hit by torpedoes.

He raced down again to dress and was back on the bridge, calculating how to save the ship. Eight minutes after the torpedoes had hit, his second-in-command arrived on the bridge with a damage report: he suggested that they should abandon ship. Despite the fact that *Indianapolis* was keeling over increasingly, McVay was dulled with sleep and believed that they could limp home, as they had from Okinawa. But he trusted the judgement of his executive officer and gave the order. He also ordered that they should send an urgent distress signal with their position. This was another crucial moment for his court martial a few months later.

Because *Indianapolis* was equipped as a flagship, there were two radio huts aboard. It seems likely that none of the messages sent out by the main radio station got through, but the rear shack was hastily repaired and the signal went out. What happened next would be debated for the rest of the century and beyond. For a long time, the naval authorities believed that no distress signal had been received – many of the senior officers believed that none had even been sent. But it became clear later that at least two of these signals had been picked up in Leyte. One was received by a radio operator who took it straight to the relevant officer in charge of operations at Leyte, who was asleep. The operator would suggest later that there was a strong smell of alcohol in the room.

A second distress signal was received elsewhere in the same dockyard and, on his own authority, the officer on duty dispatched two tugs to the position to search for survivors. In the morning, both tugs were recalled by his superior officer, furious that the tugs had been sent without his consent, because the distress signal had not been confirmed.

These incidents have never been fully explained, and they go to the heart of why *Indianapolis* disappeared. It is worth explaining that, while the centralised authority and deference in the US navy was not as pronounced as it was for

Hashimoto and the Japanese, the American naval tradition does not favour the creative disobeying of orders, as Nelson's legacy did for the British navy. An American commanding officer had less leeway than his British opposite number to act on his own initiative. This does not explain how a cruiser the size of *Indianapolis* was allowed to disappear – there were rigidities and deference in the British navy that also led to disasters – but it does explain a little about how hard it was for the authorities in Leyte to act promptly.

In their defence too, the Japanese navy had been sending out bogus distress signals designed precisely to lure ships out of harbour into the path of submarines, which made them suspicious of distress signals – especially as the information that *Indianapolis* was on its way had also not been received. But equally, no attempt seems to have been made to work out whether this distress signal, on which so many lives depended, was genuine or not. Lieutenant Commander Jules Sancho and Lieutenant Stewart Gibson, in charge of the routings at Leyte were both new in their posts, and had also been struggling with re-routing ships around a serious cyclone to the north. Their commanding officer, Commodore Norman Gillette, was only looking after things for a temporary posting. Their assumption, if they knew about the distress signals – and most did not – was that a ship the size of *Indianapolis* would have time to confirm before it went down.

In fact, there were only four minutes left between the order to abandon ship and the disappearance of *Indianapolis* beneath the waves, so there was little enough time to send more than a few signals before the radio operators and their equipment had slid off onto the bulkhead as the ship began to heel over.

Many of the crew were already in the sea, knocked overboard by the explosion or the serious list to starboard. Those which fell in the sea on the right hand side were able to collect the lifejackets and other bits and pieces of wreckage. On the other hand, they also had to contend with the ship looming above them and threatening to crush them as it fell. McVay himself was knocked overboard by a large wave and found himself drifting near the propellers, which were still spinning in the air. He swam out of the way as fast as he could and, when he looked back, the ship had gone. It had been only twelve minutes since the torpedoes hit.

About 300 of the ship's crew of 1,200 were already dead, killed in the explosions or trapped below deck when the ship sank. About half the 900 or so in the water had lifejackets, though they also knew that the fuel oil in the water would begin to corrode them and split the seams if they were in the sea too long. There had been no time to organise an orderly evacuation and certainly no time to launch life-rafts or distribute provisions or water supplies.

McVay was not actually in touch with the vast majority of the survivors in the water. He was near a smaller group. He was also uninjured and was lucky enough to find a potato crate and then a raft, and then another one. He was able to lash them together and take other survivors out of the sea. He began to repeat his mantra which he repeated many times in the next few days: don't worry, we will be rescued, don't lose faith, keep heart.

In fact, of course, they were in the middle of the biggest ocean in the world, and McVay was only too aware that the distress signals had probably not been sent, let alone picked up. It might be necessary to wait until *Indianapolis* failed to arrive in Leyte for the alarm to be raised. That was a long time to be on the ocean with no food or water, in the searing heat of the day and the freezing temperatures at night. But he kept his doubts to himself, staying sane by keeping a makeshift log on pieces of borrowed paper recording the planes they could see hurtling overhead. They tried to attract the attention of the pilots with a mirror, flashing the light into the cockpit. It didn't work. He will have known how difficult it was to catch sight of a man in the water from the air, even if you were actually looking for him; but if you were hardly expecting anyone to be there – well, then, a sighting was extremely unlikely.

The other, bigger groups of survivors, led by the ship's doctor, Lewis Haynes – a member of Spruance's staff and one of the heroes of the sinking – were in an even more desperate position, in the water, with the injured and dying around them, and also without provisions or anything to drink. Haynes and the chaplain, Thomas Conway, led prayers for rescue.

On board I-58, Hashimoto had two immediate concerns. His crew were nervous about a depth charge attack in response to their obvious success – Hashimoto had not seen *Indianapolis* sink through the periscope, nor seen any wreckage or people in the water. But he did not believe it was possible for a ship that badly damaged to have escaped so fast. He believed the target had been sunk, but he also needed to reassure his crew that the target had been alone on the ocean.

A less immediate problem was posed by the *kaiten* pilots. They had long since accepted the inevitability of their death, and had become fanatical exponents of the sacrificial, suicide approach. But since they were going to die, they wanted to do so in the most worthwhile way. The idea that they had missed the chance of sinking what they believed to have been an enemy battleship was deeply disappointing. And their commitment had undermined the traditional deference in any navy for the captain – he was beset by shouted suggestions and entreaties throughout the attack on *Indianapolis*. One of them, in particular, was now in tears. Hashimoto had to calm his kaiten crews and reassure them that there would be other targets soon.

That night, the crew of I-58 celebrated their victory with their favourite meal: rice with tinned beans, boiled eels and corned beef.

After I-58 had left the scene, the survivors found themselves drifting, though they had no equipment to measure it. McVay in particular drifted over a hundred miles in the next five days. Their initial hopes of rescue had long since been dashed and it was clear the pilots on their way to Guam were unable to see them and remained unaware of them. In McVay's mind, and all those in the water, the calculations were going on about how long before it would be clear that *Indianapolis* was overdue in Leyte, and how long they could at least expect the search to begin. The various hopes for clean water or brandy supplies had also evaporated. Both McVay and Haynes had tested bottles only to find they were impregnated with sea water and had to be thrown away. McVay was so concerned to keep up morale that he lied that one cracked water cask should be kept until they were really desperate.

The heat was intense, and the wounded were now dying. Fr Conway, the chaplain, was kept busy conducting makeshift funeral services. Then, at dusk on the second day (31 July), the nightmare really began. The blood in the water and the bodies had attracted the great horror for sailors. By the time the implacable sun dipped below the horizon again, they found they were surrounded by a large group of sharks from various species. They were visible in the distance and, in their delirious state, some of the men thought they were patrol boats. They waited through the night and, at dawn, the sharks moved in.

In the morning light on the third day (1 August) the first people in the water began to disappear. These are controversial stories even now, and the testimony of survivors is divided between those who saw living sailors taken by sharks in the water and those that did not, and in fact suggested that the sharks were testing whether or not they were dead: one of those was Dr Haynes. "When the night came, things would bump against you in the dark or brush against your leg," he wrote later, "but honestly, in the entire 110 hours that I was in the water, I did not see a man attacked by a shark."

These days, most authorities suggest that people approached by sharks should stay completely still, because thrashing will attract them. But this was not a situation the men in the water had been trained for and they thrashed like mad, partly to show the sharks they were still alive. There were, after all, enough bodies in the water to attract the sharks and the next morning a number of them were found partly eaten. There was the horrific experience, which a number of the survivors remembered, of prodding a friend to make sure they were still alive, only to have the body fall over in the water because they had been eaten in half below the waterline.

That same morning, events were taking place in Leyte which might have made the remaining survivors despair, if they had known about it. The busy operations officer in charge of the plotting board there, Captain Alfred Granum, tracking the ships' across their region of the ocean, moved *Indianapolis* onto the 'arrived' list. He assumed that is what had happened, not having heard anything to the contrary. The same thing also happened in Guam. There was one other relevant list, that of the ships in harbour in Leyte, which marked *Indianapolis* as overdue. But Gibson in Leyte assumed, quite reasonably, that – as a flagship – *Indianapolis* had been ordered elsewhere.

Again, this all also requires some explanation, beyond the kind of bureaucratic inertia which tends to take over when the risk is considered negligible and when momentous events tended to be happening elsewhere. In fact, as a move to reduce bureaucracy, naval authorities had been told to stop reporting when ships had arrived safely. It was assumed by most of those responsible for the busy port that *Indianapolis* had simply docked.

Perhaps those in the water sensed that they had been forgotten and that their ship, against all expectations, had been allowed simply to disappear. Perhaps it was no coincidence that, on the same day (1 August), the suicides began. Some of those maddened by the desire for water, would go quiet for a few hours, then they would lie back, swim a couple of strokes away, and then just disappear. By then, most of the survivors with broken limbs had gone into shock and died.

But then there was a less pleasant way to decide to die. Haynes, the ship's doctor, had been tireless in his determination to prevent the men around him from drinking sea water. He knew only too well, what the effects of salt poisoning would be: elation, followed by collapse, delirium, and screaming. Through the night, you could hear the wails of those who had drunk sea water, as well as those who were being taken – or thought they were being taken – by the sharks. It was a vision of hell and it was only getting worse. The chaplain resisted the sea water but was still among those who died. Those who survived found a different way of dealing with it. "At first you get in a situation where you abhor it," said Haynes later. "You can't stand it, it's terrible, but you can't get away from it, so you stick with it. And then you get so that you tolerate it. You tolerate it long enough, you embrace it, it becomes your way of life."

On Tuesday night, McVay gathered his immediate group, about four miles from the main group of survivors, and said the Lord's Prayer. As it turned out, Tuesday night was the worst so far. Dr Haynes took up the story:

"The water in that part of the Pacific was warm and good for swimming. But body temperature is over 98 and when you immerse someone up to their chin in that water for a couple of days. You're going to chill him down. So at night, we would tie everyone close together to stay warm. But they still had severe chills which led to fever and delirium. On Tuesday night, some guy began yelling 'There's a Jap here and he's trying to kill me.' And then everybody started to fight. They were totally out of their minds. A lot of men were killed that night. A lot of men drowned. Overnight, everybody untied themselves and got scattered in all directions. But you couldn't blame the men. It was mass hysteria. You became wary of everyone. Till daylight came, you weren't sure. When we got back together the next day there were a hell of a lot fewer. There were also mass hallucinations. It was amazing how everyone would see the same thing. One would see something, then someone else would see it. One day, everyone got in a long line. I said: 'What are you doing?' Someone answered: 'Doctor, there's an island up here just ahead of us. One of us can go ashore at a time and you can get fifteen minutes sleep.' They all saw the island. You couldn't convince them otherwise."

Delirium could take people n different ways. On one occasion, many of those in the water became convinced that *Indianapolis* lay just below them in the water and the canteen was still open. On another occasion, one survivor gouged out the eyes of another with his bare hands. It isn't clear whether anyone in the water could have survived another night, if I had not been for Chuck Gwinn.

Lieutenant Chuck Gwinn, based on Peleliu Island on a PV-1, a Lockheed Ventura patrol aircraft, flew over at 11.25 in the morning of the fourth day (2 August). He was flying at 3,000 feet just over a hundred miles since the position where *Indianapolis* had gone down, and was trying to fix the planes new antenna. It was then that he sighted an oil slick and assumed, since he had heard of no American sinkings, that it must have come from a damaged Japanese submarine. Investigating more closely, he spotted people in the water, circled and dropped a life-raft and supplies. Unsure who they were, he reported to his headquarters on Peleliu that he had seen 30 survivors in the water. It was the first independent report of the sinking of the *Indianapolis*.

Circling back over the area, Gwinn had soon counted over a hundred heads in the water. This meant that they could not be Japanese. There was little or no Japanese merchant shipping left at this stage in the war and certainly not here, and he knew perfectly well that no Japanese submarines carried a crew of more than a hundred. It had to be American.

On Peleliu, Lieutenant Commander George Atteberry received the message and, on his own authority, ordered a Catalina flying board to take over from Gwinn, without waiting for official confirmation. But the duty officer wanted to wait for official confirmation, and Atteberry realised a Catalina would take too long to get there and Gwinn would have to fly home before it arrived. So he refuelled a bomber from his own squadron and took off. It was this kind of behaviour, in defiance of procedure and sometimes orders, which made the effective rescue possible. The commander in

Guam, Vice-Admiral George Murray, immediately ordered two destroyers to sea. But what turned out to be the crucial intervention was by Lieutenant Adrian Marks, who had deciphered Gwinn's original message and loaded up with life-rafts and had taken off from Peleliu Island, again on his own authority.

The final critical piece of the story of rescue came with another case of a confident officer ignoring protocols. Captain Graham Claytor was actually a cousin of McVay's wife Louise, though he had no reason at that stage to imagine that this had anything to do with the *Indianapolis*. He was then only 200 miles away, in command of the destroyer *Cecil J. Doyle*. As soon as he overheard Marks' radio reports, he turned the ship around without waiting for orders, and headed for the survivors at speed. Granum on Leyte guessed the link with the overdue *Indianapolis* and broke radio silence to ask ships to state their position in the area. As he feared, no reply came from *Indianapolis*.

When Marks arrived in his Catalina, he could see there were hundreds of sharks now circling the survivors. Marks realised that there was really no time to wait. He radioed to Peleliu what turned out to be the most famous signal of the affair:

"Will attempt sea landing."

This was in explicit defiance of the regulations. Landing in the open sea was expressly forbidden, because most attempts had ended in disaster. But Marks had seen the sharks and took a vote among his own crew that, despite a twelve foot swell, they would try to get down. There was a tricky series of bumps, and they were bobbing around in the Pacific. Marks put his crewman Morgan Hensley, an amateur wrestler, on the port side, and moved towards the stragglers, guided from the air by Atteberry. By nightfall on Wednesday, Marks had collected 56 survivors, and when the fuselage was full, he had wrapped the rest in parachutes and put them on the wings.

Cecil J. Doyle arrived at 11.45 that night. Claytor launched their motor boat to pick up the survivors, asking them what ship they were from. In fact, it was Claytor who first sent a signal to senior commanders that he was "picking up survivors of the USS *Indianapolis*, torpedoed and sunk last Sunday night". In the darkness, he also disobeyed orders – and took a major risk – by shining his ship's searchlight directly upwards, so that they could be seen by rescue planes and boats, and crucially by survivors still in the water.

"After midnight, a little bit before, there was a light shining off the bottom of the cloud and we knew then we were saved, wrote crewman Woody Eugene. "That was the spotlight of the *Cecil Doyle*. The navy is on the scene. There's a ship coming. You can't believe how happy we were, guys screaming and yelling 'We're saved, we're saved!'"

In all, ten ships and a number of planes were involved in searching a hundred square miles in the days that followed. McVay was among the last to be rescued, by the transport ship *Ringness*. He had been on the raft four and a half days without food or water.

Some hundreds of miles to the north west, Hashimoto was picking up frenetic wireless traffic. The rescue was clearly under way. This was the biggest air-sea rescue operation of the war, just as it was probably the biggest recorded attack by sharks on human beings. In both cases, the statistics were borrowed by the US navy, horrified that this disaster should have been allowed to happen and quick to demonstrate their own energy against impossible natural odds. This damage limitation operation had only just begun, and it would become notorious.

Chapter 4
An aftermath

"I think they're going to put it to me."
**Captain Charles McVay to one of his fellow
survivors, Peleliu Island**

The sea rescue would continue for more than a
week, and – after the last survivor had been taken
on board, cleaned up and given a little water (too
much would have been dangerous after that length
of time without) – there was the task of collecting
the bodies and, where possible, identifying them.
About a quarter of the bodies in the water, just
over fifty of them, were found to have been
mutilated by sharks.

On Peleliu Island, where most of the survivors
had been taken, there was a news blackout.
Guards were posted on the hospital block where
the survivors were recovering. The navy
authorities were extremely nervous about how the
story would affect their reputation, and – as a
handful of the elite knew – in what was probably
the final weeks of the war. On 5 August, McVay
was allowed to give a news conference, but subject

to naval censorship, in which he asked pointedly why it was not clear to the authorities that *Indianapolis* had been overdue.

The following morning, at 8.15 Tokyo time, the black canister they had carried to Tinian Island was put into terrifying use, after two letters by nuclear scientists begging Truman not to do so without warning had been considered and rejected. The Enola Gay Superfortress dropped the bomb named 'Little Boy' on the city of Hiroshima. After technical problems carrying a bomb of that weight – three B-29 bombers carrying the same load as the atomic bomb crashed on take-off – Enola Gay took off from a specially lengthened runway in the early hours, seven tons too heavy. The crew had waited three days for the weather to clear.

On board were four hand-picked scientists and a crew of nine who had been training together for a year. Only the captain, Paul Tibbets, knew what kind of bomb they were carrying was. Just after 8am, the crew could see Hiroshima ahead and put on special arc-welder's goggles to protect their eyes. Just 51 seconds after it was dropped, it exploded just less than 2,000 feet above the city. From fifteen miles away, Tibbets could see a ball of fire – with the temperature for a brief moment of one million degrees and 6,000 degrees immediately below on the ground, together with the terrifying and now familiar grey mushroom cloud.

"The surface was nothing but a black, boiling … barrel of tar," he said. "Where before there had been a city – distinctive houses, buildings and everything, that you could see from our altitude – now you couldn't see anything except black boiling debris down below."

In seconds, the fireball had vaporised thousands of people in the centre of Hiroshima, leaving their shadows scorched into the walls behind them and charred tens of thousands more. The shock wave which followed – with a force of eight tons per square yard – flattened buildings, tore clothes and skin from bodies, and annihilated the whole commercial and residential centre of the city. Now as much as 360 miles away, the crew of the Enola Gay could still see the mushroom cloud over the city. Between 71,000 and 80,000 people were killed instantly in the blast: estimates of the total dead, including those from radiation, range from 160,000 to 240,000.

The people of Hiroshima had been generally spared by the bombers, but they had been expecting a serious raid. Every night they had been queuing up with their carts to leave, but even so the population was still 300,000. Nearly all those within half a mile of the epicentre who survived the blast died from the effects of radiation. Before that many of them had been completely disorientated by the blast and the disappearance of their city, finding their way by tramlines past the screaming and dying animals and people, hundreds of them writhing in agony with their whole faces burned away

It became known later that the technicians had chalked on the side of the bomb after assembly the words: "This one is for the boys of the *Indianapolis*".

Two days later, Stalin finally put his own plans into effect. Soviet forces overran the Japanese fortress of Hutou in Manchuria, and American bombers hit a series of naval bases on the Japanese mainland. By the end of fighting, the Russians had advanced 250 miles and their troops were ashore on Sakhalin and Kurile islands.

Then, on 9 August, a second atomic bomb was dropped on the city of Nagasaki. Japanese ministers had no means of knowing how many more bombs were available, but they were still deadlocked about what to do next. It was left to Hirohito to break out of his normally silent role, with the instruction to his ministers that "the unendurable must be endured". On 14 August, Japan agreed to surrender, with the single condition that the emperor's position should be preserved.

Hirohito recorded a radio announcement, and that night young extremist officers broke into his palace, killing the general in command but failing to find the recording, which had been hidden in the basement. It was broadcast the following morning. Hirohito's voice had never been heard publicly before, and he spoke the strange flowery language of the court, so most listeners did not understand what he was saying.

The day of the Emperor's broadcast, I-58 was at sea near Okinawa. The crew were elated after a successful attack on an American merchant ship the day before, where kaiten had been used (American naval experts tended to be sceptical about this, because they claimed it was a way for Hashimoto to cover up the fact that *Indianapolis* had been sunk by a kaiten torpedo, though he always disputed this). Hashimoto was standing on the conning tower when his wireless rating asked him to come downstairs. "I thought I had never seen a man look so sad," he wrote later. "He looked ready to burst into tears at any minute."

Hashimoto was taken to a corner of the wardroom where he was shown a copy of the Emperor's communiqué. "I felt stunned, but after considering for a moment, I decided it could only be some newspaper stunt, not an official signal. Taking a grip on myself, I said: 'This may be a broadcast for the purposes of a demarché (a foreign intervention). Destroy it and throw it away'."

One of his officers overheard. "If this is a demarché, it's a very skilful one," he said. Hashimoto decided not to tell the crew, in case it led to some kind of accident – a huge risk with a submarine – and he asked for all signal messages to be brought straight to him. Only once they had reached Kure, with the crew lined up before him, did Hashimoto read the imperial despatch out loud to them, with tears running down his face. Then, without a word, he stepped into the motor launch to take him to the submarine base.

Once the Emperor had made his broadcast, President Truman spoke to the US nation by wireless at 7pm on 14 August (15 August in Japan). Immediately before he started speaking on the air, the White House issued the official statement about the loss of the *Indianapolis*. Some families of the crew members got the news about the sinking and the end of the war at the very same time.

Even after the surrender, the war was not quite at an end. Hashimoto reports huge arguments among the officers at his naval base. There were also leaflets dropped from planes urging the navy to continue the war. Allied leaflets were being dropped at the same time on prisoner of war camps all over South East Asia, explaining that the war was over and that help was on its way. Japanese officers who had executed seven American prisoners of war near Singapore were digging up their bodies to destroy the evidence. The Russians were occupying Port Arthur, which they had lost during the Russo-Japanese War in 1904, the American officer John Birch was being shot by a Chinese communist patrol, and the communist guerrilla leader Ho Chi-minh was seizing power in Indo-China.

Indo-China had been under complete Japanese control since March, when they had slaughtered the French garrisons there. The 20th Indian Division entered Saigon on 13 September, and

French troops arrived shortly afterwards and began a civil war against the Viet Minh which was to last in one form or another until the Vietnam War.

On 28 August, members of MacArthur's staff landed near Yokohama to begin the occupation – the first Allies to set foot on mainland Japan – unsure how they would be received. It took MacArthur two weeks to reach Japan from Manila, but once there he took the formal surrender on 2 September in Tokyo Bay on the deck of the battleship *Missouri* – a subtle tribute to Truman, whose home state was Missouri. Behind him stood General Arthur Percival, a prisoner since the fall of Singapore, and General Jonathan Wainwright who had been a prisoner since the fall of Bataan, both looking ill and skeletally thin.

Meanwhile, McVay began to fear the worst. "I think they're going to put it to me," he told one of his fellow survivors in Peleliu.

It was certainly clear that the navy could not just ignore their biggest wartime loss of life. A hastily arranged court of inquiry blamed the disaster on the failure to send a distress signal – McVay told them he believed there had been no time for the signal to be sent – and on his failure to zigzag despite the moonlit conditions. It recommended that he be court martialled. The navy then also charged him with failing to abandon ship a timely manner. This was necessary for the court martial to go ahead, because McVay accepted that the signals had not been sent and freely admitted that *Indianapolis* had not been zigzagging. The navy wanted to be seen to be holding someone to account, and that meant there had to be some issue of dispute.

The war was over. The one thing the naval command wanted to do was to bask in the glory of a difficult and dangerous task achieved, and then this enormous mistake emerged just when it was least helpful. *Time* magazine described it as a "colossal blunder" by the navy. The press was in full cry. So when McVay's court martial sat in December, in Washington Navy Yard, it was open to the media and the public, and they turned out in full force to see the guilty punished.

It was also increasingly clear to the naval prosecutors that the case was not exactly clear cut. It was not widely known, for example, that the navy had access to information which could have been passed on to McVay. The destroyer *Underhill* had been sunk on the same route on 24 July, just five days before *Indianapolis*. Senior naval intelligence officials also knew from decrypt intelligence that I-58 had left Kure.

It also seemed likely that *Indianapolis* had not actually disappeared at all, but had simply been mislaid by the navy. It was clear that Hashimoto had sent a signal to Tokyo that he had hit a battleship of the Idaho class, and it had definitely sunk. This was decoded and sent to Guam where it as ignored.

The navy decided to withhold a secret report which admitted that they had failed to use decrypt intelligence which strongly suggested there had been submarine activity on the Guam-Leyte route. Naval officials in Guam also accepted that McVay had been told that the threat from submarines was "practically negligible".

The prosecutors were also about to bring a wholly unexpected element to bear in the court martial. As an officer in a defeated navy, with his nation under occupation, Hashimoto was in effect a prisoner-of-war. If the Americans wanted him to give evidence in their court martial, they could simply instruct him to do so. So early in December 1945, he was put on a transport plane and a train across the USA, to Washington Navy Yard.

When he arrived in the capital city of his recent enemies, Hashimoto was clearly uncomfortable. The national press and the politicians were outraged that so recent an enemy was being flown in to give evidence against a decorated American naval officer. It was as if the sinking was just the first damage, that Hashimoto was somehow being encouraged to torpedo McVay all over again.

He looked even more uncomfortable in the witness box, where he spent 50 minutes in a crowded court room and where he was provided with a naval interpreter – though actually he did speak a little English – and was asked about the visibility on the night, five months before, when *Indianapolis* had gone down.

This was to be a continuing source of controversy in the years that followed. In his witness statement, Hashimoto had said that it would have made no difference if his target had been zigzagging. Expert witnesses were also called to give evidence that zigzagging was only rarely a useful defence against submarines. But when it came to the cross-examination, Hashimoto's evidence was less clear. He said that, if *Indianapolis* had been zigzagging, it would have involved no change in the method of firing the torpedoes but some changes in manoeuvring.

This was more equivocal and it left an element of doubt. Hashimoto was aware, also, that his answer had not been translated quite as he intended, because his English extended that far. But he felt, as a prisoner-of-war, he was in no position to protest to the judge. But for the rest of his life, he claimed that his evidence had been mistranslated.

"I understood English a little bit even then, so I could see at the time I testified that the translator did not tell fully what I said," said Hashimoto later. "I mean it was not because of the capacity of the translator. I would say the Navy side did not accept some testimony that was inconvenient to them ... I was then an officer of the beaten country, you know, and alone, how could I complain strongly enough?... At the time of the court martial, I had a feeling that it was contrived from the beginning."

After two weeks of evidence, it was clear that there was no evidence that McVay had failed to give the order to abandon ship in good time, but the failure to zigzag charge stuck. This is the official communiqué put out by the Navy Department after the decision, not just about McVay but about the naval officials at Leyte and Guam, Gillette, Granum, Sancho and Gibson.

"The following disciplinary action has been taken in connection with the loss of the *Indianapolis*:

Captain Charles B. McVay, III, USN, has been brought to trial by General Court Martial. He was acquitted of failure to give timely orders to abandon ship. He was found guilty of negligence in not causing a zigzag to be steered. He was sentenced to lose one hundred numbers in his temporary grade of Captain and also in his permanent grade of Commander. The Court and also the Commander in Chief, United States Fleet recommended clemency. The Secretary of the Navy has approved these recommendations, remitted the sentence, and restored Captain McVay to duty.

The Secretary of the Navy has given Commodore N.C. Gillette, USN, a Letter of Reprimand, which will become part of his permanent official record.

The Secretary of the Navy has given Captain A.M. Granum, USN, a Letter of Reprimand, which will become part of his permanent official record.

The Commander in Chief, Pacific Fleet has given Lieutenant Commander Jules C. Sancho, USNR, a Letter of Admonition, which will become part of his permanent official record.

The Commander in Chief, Pacific Fleet has given Lieutenant Stuart B. Gibson, USNR, a Letter of Reprimand, which will become part of his permanent official record."

In the months that followed, the Navy Secretary James Forrestal removed the letters of reprimand from the other officers, restored McVay to the active list, but left the record on McVay's file. Other navies in the world have different methods of testing the events around sinkings, even in wartime. The British navy court martialled the commanding officer of a ship that is lost as a matter of course until just before the First World War, but the US navy did not. So not only was McVay the only captain in the US Navy ever court martialled for losing his ship by enemy action, but he was the only officer to sustain continuing criticism of his conduct over the whole business of the disappearance of the *Indianapolis.*

It was Christmas just days after the end of the court martial, and the first pieces of hate mail were received by McVay from the families of crew members. He was to carry on receiving them for the rest of his life. He was reassigned to a desk job at a naval air station but, despite the reprimand, be continued to progress in his naval career.

Hashimoto had been stunned by the way he was treated during the trial, actually with great honour, though he had been confined to his navy dormitory while he was in Washington. When he was back in Japan he became a demobilization officer in the naval section of the Ministry of Demobilization, taking apart what little remained of the Japanese navy. He became a civilian in June 1946, and wrote a book seven years later about the Japanese submarine service. It was called *Sunk* and, although it was hardly bitter, it was critical of a naval establishment which had been too authoritarian, and too jealous, to learn vital technical and strategic lessons.

By 1960, McVay had retired from the navy as a rear-admiral. That was the year he attended a crew reunion for the first time in the city of Indianapolis and was cheered by the remaining survivors. His wife Louise, the sister of Graham Claytor of the *Cecil J. Doyle,* died of cancer in 1961. McVay remarried but never quiet recovered. His grandson died in 1965, which hit him hard, and still the hate letters kept coming.

In November 1968, he shot himself in his

garden in Litchfield, Connecticut, a hundred miles outside New York City. He had been having nightmares about his time on the makeshift raft, and Christmas was approaching, which would inevitably bring more unpleasant letters from the relatives of those who had died. He was found by the back porch clutching a sailor doll, which his father had given him.

The death toll of the sinking of the *Indianapolis* made it the US navy's worst disaster at sea – 880 died out of a crew of 1,197 on board at the time – but because the news emerged the day the war ended, it effectively buried the story. It would be three decades before memories were revived in the minds of the public, when the 1975 film *Jaws* reminded people of the horror of those days lost at sea. One of the characters, Captain Quint, turns out to have been among the survivors in the water, and he has a horrific story to tell about the sharks – also launching a controversy about whether the sharks had actually attacked the living or just the dead.

In fact, it was watching *Jaws* in the summer of 1996 when an eleven-year-old from Pensacola High School in Florida called Hunter Scott listened to the testimony of Captain Quint. "As I listened to the story of the men being attacked by sharks, I was fascinated," Scott wrote later. "I had heard what Quint said before, but this was the first time I had really listened."

He asked his father, a high school principle, whether the story was true. "Yes," said his father, "and please move from in front of the TV."

Scott made it the subject for his history project but, even though his father took him to the local university library, he could find almost no information. He advertised in the local naval newspaper – and Pensacola is a naval town in Florida – and tracked down a survivor called Maurice Bell, and interviewed him. At that stage, as it turned out, 154 of the 317 survivors were still alive. Hunter Scott found others and they all told him about what they considered the injustice done to McVay. In 1997, Scott wrote to the president (then Bill Clinton) and the navy secretary John Dalton and set out to win the national history competition so that his project would be displayed in Washington.

His entry was disqualified on a technicality – he wasn't allowed to include notebooks – but by then he had received an extraordinary response from the survivors. The news also reached local congressman Joe Scarborough. One thing led to another and soon his project was featuring on

NBC *Nightly News* and Scott was invited as guest of honour to the next survivors' reunion in Indianapolis.

Scarborough drafted the first of three pieces of legislation designed to exonerate McVay and a former *Indianapolis* crewman, the lobbyist Mike Monroney who missed the final trip, came out of retirement to make the bill law. By now the story was being covered

on the front of the *New York Times*. People from all over the world were sending him scraps of information, some of them addressed simply to 'Hunter Scott, Pensacola, Florida'.

Hashimoto had also met the survivors. He had always been a religious man and, when he retired, he became a Shinto priest – like his father – at a shrine in the ancient city of Kyoto. In 1990, he was invited to meet survivors in Pearl Harbour. He told them, again through an interpreter: "I came here to pray with you for your shipmates whose deaths I caused."

One of the survivors, Giles McCoy, had become a kind of spokesperson for the group. "I forgive you," he said.

But it was through a Japanese journalist that Hashimoto became involved in the story one final time. In 1999, she told him about Hunter Scott's campaign and how the Senate Armed Services Committee had become involved as part of the process of legislation. Hashimoto said he would like to help and asked Scott what he could do. Scott suggested that he write a letter to the committee chair, Senator John Warner. This is what he wrote:

"I do not understand why Captain McVay was court-martialled. I do not understand why he was convicted on the charge of hazarding his ship by failing to zigzag because I would have been able to launch a successful torpedo attack against his ship whether it had been zigzagging or not. I have met many of your brave men who survived the sinking of the *Indianapolis*. I would like to join them in urging that your national legislature clear their captain's name. Our peoples have forgiven each other for that terrible war and its consequences. Perhaps it is time your people forgave Captain McVay for the humiliation of his unjust conviction."

The hearings were taking place now that the legislation exonerating McVay had been introduced for the third time. This time, the wording said clearly that the court martial had been flawed, and its findings were "morally not sustainable", leading to the "unjust humiliation" of McVay.

As well as the explosive letter from Hashimoto, Scott had managed to collect a letter from a crewman on board a landing craft at Leyte who confirmed receiving two distress signals from *Indianapolis*, both dismissed as hoaxes because they had not been confirmed – though the reason they had not been confirmed was that the ship had taken only twelve minutes to sink. But he also heard from the same witness that a senior naval officer had come on board six weeks later, and removed a large section of their logbook. This was clear evidence of a cover-up, anyway among the officers on Leyte.

Another letter confirmed that a senior officer there had been informed about the distress signal from *Indianapolis,* and ignored it, and remembered there being a "strong odour of alcohol in the room". It also confirmed the rumour that two rescue tugs had indeed been sent, and then recalled.

The hearing itself culminated in a stand-off between Admiral Donald Pilling, the vice chief of naval operations, and the Republican senator Bob Smith of New Hampshire. Pilling claimed that

McVay had not actually been convicted of losing his ship, but simply for his failure to zigzag. This is what Smith said:

"Suppose all 1,197 men came into port alive, the ship is in good shape, no four days of shark attacks, no exposure to weather and the water, no fires, no botched search, no botched recovery effort, no botched withholding of evidence, not informing of enemy message traffic. And upon arrival of the crew and the ship, one of these men, or one of their colleagues, made a request to the navy that said Captain McVay did not zigzag ... you're telling me he would have been court martialled?"

In October 2000, the resolution finally passed though the Senate, more than three years since the process had been launched by Hunter Scott's school project. Five days before, Mochitsura Hashimoto died in Kyoto at the age of 91.

The process of formally clearing Charles McVay's name was actually to take another nine months. The following July, the US navy reported that they had no legal power to remove documentation from the personnel files of dead officers, but that they would add the Senate resolution to McVay's file to "address the false perception that he had been somehow responsible for the tragedy".

Chapter 5
A conclusion

"The best laid schemes o' mice an' men
Gang aft a-gley..."
Robert Burns, 'To a mouse'

The story of the *Indianapolis* is not just about the tragedy of lives lost, though the sinking and its aftermath was certainly a tragedy. It is the story also of a sideshow, a small by-product of the enormous operation to develop, test, transport and finally to drop, the first atomic bomb ever used in anger – with the most devastating consequences for those who were in Hiroshima at the time, and for later generations. Whatever the arguments about whether or not it should have been used – and there are still points to be made on both sides – the fates of both the city of Hiroshima and of the cruiser *Indianapolis* are, in some ways, also both aspects of the same huge tragedy: the Second World War and the Pacific war.

It is also a reminder of how disasters happen, when suddenly the fates seem to align and so many elements – so unlikely in combination – come together in unpredictable ways. If McVay had been given the information he needed, if the moon had not shone at that precise moment – before the captain had been warned – if McVay had not been asleep, if *Indianapolis* was not in precisely that position at that time, if Hashimoto had not calculated correctly with the wrong information about his target: so many ifs, but all of them happened.

If the information received on Leyte and Guam had been believed – if more officers had taken a little more of a risk with protocol and deference, as Adrian Marks and Graham Claytor did – then the ship need not have disappeared. But the combination did arise and it did disappear.

It is possible to go further back too: if the kamikaze had missed *Indianapolis* in March 1945. If the cruiser *Pensacola* had not broken down. If McVay had insisted on an escort. The best laid schemes of mice and men are not proof against such eventualities, and – if the fate had not befallen *Indianapolis* – perhaps it would have been another ship that sank.

But there is another aspect of these events which

are interesting for another reason – for the light they shine on the question of how organisations, navies or nations, learn to become more effective.

Perhaps one of the saddest elements in Hashimoto's book was one of the notes left behind after his death by a kaiten pilot, who realised he was about to sacrifice his life, when those who had ordered him to do so did not provide him with the intelligence data he needed to make his death worthwhile. He was about to go into Guam harbour, at the beginning of 1945, launched from I-58, without aerial reconnaissance:

"Was it not irresponsible to send us into the attack without giving us some idea of the enemy's defences or the conditions inside the harbour?"

Hashimoto hated sending them to their deaths with just a bland reassurance that an aircraft carrier might be there when they arrived, but what could he do? He had already been fighting a long battle with the naval authorities about his right to innovate a workable radar for himself. Even on that voyage, to Guam, he was surprised on the surface by aircraft and realised the sets still did not work effectively. What frustrated him was not just the deference endemic in the Imperial Japanese command, but the ruinous inter-departmental rivalries and pride which were putting his life and all his men at risk.

In exile in England at the time, the Viennese philosopher Karl Popper was about to publish his monumental work *The Open Society and its Enemies*, in which he explained why 'open societies' – where it was possible to challenge from lower ranks or the front line – could learn and innovate and develop better than closed ones. Put like that, the greater openness of the allied forces explained one reason why the war in the Pacific was won by one side rather than another. Popper explained why authoritarian tyrannies were not actually very effective. Closed societies can delude themselves; open societies still can, but they tend to delude themselves less.

So when the former fleet chief of staff Admiral Shigeru Fukutome asked himself after the war, how the Japanese submarine fleet could have deluded itself so badly, this provides some of the answer. "They considered themselves superior in technique in the field of submarine warfare to any in other navies," he wrote. "But when it came to the test of actual warfare, the results were deplorable."

But the *Indianapolis* sinking revealed that the US navy was not immune to this kind of thinking, where the dignity of the organisation, or its parts, or of key officers involved, became more important than the fate of individuals – where rescue tugs were recalled just because they had not been ordered to sea in the approved method. Or where, to use the most extreme example, officials could remove pages from logbooks which might threaten the navy's case.

The US navy underwent a huge change between 1942 and 1945. Halsey and Spruance had taken James Doolittle to raid Tokyo in 1942, relying on intuition and improvisation, according to Halsey's biographer John Wukovits. But as many as 45 admirals took part in the invasion of Okinawa. There were systems and protocols to follow, and difficult hierarchies to navigate. The bureaucracy had a life of its own and it didn't like criticism.

This was the background to the humiliation of Captain McVay. The case was not cut and dried. There was an issue about the failure of the *Indianapolis* to resume zigzagging once the moon had risen – a question, not whether he had disobeyed orders by not zigzagging at night, but whether he had actually *intended* not to do so in moonlight, whether he had left orders to change tack if the visibility changed. In the end, the zigzagging would have made no difference, yet the navy needed an example to be made to obscure the fact that they had allowed one of the most famous ships in the fleet to disappear, and left their crew floating in the Pacific.

Yet the story reveals not just the combination of failures in Guam and Leyte, but the ability of individuals in the system to refuse to accept what they had been told – whether it was Graham Claytor speeding to the scene, or Adrian Marks landing on the ocean, or Hunter Scott worrying away at the issue for his high school project. Or even Mochitsura Hashimoto battling the naval authorities for a workable radar. Or of course those 300 survivors who refused to give up and clung onto life in the middle of the ocean, almost without hope and certainly without water, until they were rescued.

It reveals both the failures and the huge successes of the navy at the end of a brutal and brutalising war.

Further information and acknowledgements

I am extremely grateful to Richard Foreman and Lydia Yadi at Endeavour Press for their expert support and guidance, and to Julian Alexander and Ben Clark at Lucas Alexander Whitley, and also to the staff at the London Library for their help in the research. And to the Steyning Bookshop for sourcing so many vital books.

If you would like to find out more, some of the key texts I used included:

Buell, Thomas (2009) *The Quiet Warrior: A biography of Raymond A. Spruance*, Annapolis: Naval Institute Press (first published 1974).

Charles River Editors (2015) *The Sinking of the USS Indianapolis,* Cambridge.

Cracknell, William (1973) *USS Indianapolis (CA35), Heavy Cruiser 1931-1935*, Windsor: Profile Publications.

Harrell, David (2005), Out of the Depths,

Maitland: Xulon Press.

Harris, Brayton (2012) *Admiral Nimitz: the commander of the Pacific ocean theatre*, New York: Palgrave Macmillan.

Hashimoto, Mochitsura (2010), *Sunk: The Story of the Japanese Submarine Fleet, 1941–1945*, New York: Progressive Press (new edn.).

Nelson, Pete and Scott, Hunter (2002) *Left for Dead: A young man's search for justice for the USS Indianapolis,* New York: Delacorte Press.

Newcomb, Richard (2000), Abandon Ship!: The Saga of the USS Indianapolis, the Navy's Greatest Sea Disaster, New York: HarperCollins.

Stanton, Doug (2002) In Harm's Way: The Sinking of the USS Indianapolis and the Extraordinary Story of Its Survivors, New York, St Martin's Press.

www.ussindianapolis.org

Wukovits, John (2010) *Admiral Bull Halsey,* New York: Palgrave Macmillan.

If you enjoyed this book, you might also enjoy this by the same author:

Operation Primrose: U110, The Bismarck and the Enigma Code

It was Winston Churchill who coined the phrase 'the Battle of the Atlantic'. "Amid the torrent of violent events one anxiety reigned supreme," he wrote later, "battles might be lost or won, enterprises might succeed or miscarry, territories might be gained or quitted, but dominating all our power to carry on the war, or even keep ourselves alive, lay our mastery of the ocean routes and the free approach an entry to our ports."

Even Churchill's rotund expressions and mastery of language fails to quite do justice to the reality in mid-Atlantic, as freighters, tankers and liners were sent to the bottom in fire and burning oil, protected by an exhausted and dwindling fleet of destroyers and escorts, while increasing proportions of our imports lay in the ocean depths, along with their crews. It was a story of grit, daring, and frustration on both sides, and of long, tiring nights on watch from the sea-swept bridge of a corvette or a damp, freezing conning tower.

Meanwhile, ten more ocean-going U-boats were completing every month by the end of 1940, and the British ports were filling slowly with damaged merchant vessels that could not be repaired. In desperation, at the start of 1941, Churchill wrote a memo to the First Lord of the Admiralty, A. V. Alexander, the minister responsible for the navy, warning that cargo ships arriving in the UK that month were half those which had arrived the same month in 1940.

"How willingly would I have exchanged a full-scale attempt at invasion for this shapeless, measureless peril, expressed in charts, curves and statistics," he wrote later.

This was the reality that lay behind the desperate efforts to crack the Nazi Enigma naval code. Bletchley Park, the top secret wartime cryptography establishment, had its own stresses – but all those involved in the struggle to crack naval Enigma knew the stakes.

The performance of Benedict Cumberbatch in *The Imitation Game*, and the fascination with the life and work – and the untimely death – of Alan

Turing, has tended to throw the spotlight onto the extraordinary and secret work by these Bletchley Park code breakers. The narrative has concentrated on how the Enigma codes were cracked, and due respect has been given to all those aspects of the puzzle that came together – from the original Polish pioneers who helped to find ways of reading the early versions of Enigma and passed on their insights, and their Enigma machine, to the British, to the teams working around the clock in an obscure country house in the middle of Bedfordshire, from Turing's leaps of imagination and the beginnings of computing, to the inspirational contributions made by his colleagues which made the various steps possible.

By far the toughest aspect of cracking Enigma involved the complexities of the naval code. The army and Luftwaffe versions of Enigma succumbed to the code breakers relatively early and signals were read with increasing ease. But the naval versions still held out, for reasons that will be made clear in this short book.

The purpose of it is to tell a small slice of the story – the capture of a naval Enigma machine from U110 and its immediate consequences – but also to tell the tale in the context of one of the most important months in the business of cracking the naval Engima code, May 1941. That month saw both the capture of U110, together with an intact coding machine, just a few days after the first breakthrough – the capture of the naval Enigma settings for June – followed by the crescendo of the Battle of the Atlantic only days later: the pursuit and sinking of the German battleship *Bismarck*.

But the book has a secondary purpose. That is to try and set the story of the Enigma code-breakers at Bletchley Park back in the context from which it has been wrenched, the huge operation around naval intelligence which embedded Bletchley and the code cracking enthusiasts in Hut 8 in a wider machine that tried to use what clues were available to protect convoys, and read the minds of the enemy.

And perhaps most of all, the purpose is to set this story in the most important context of all: the fact that German code breakers had – even before the outbreak of war – been able to crack the British naval code and, while Turing and his collaborators were wrestling with the sophisticated Enigma system, their opposite numbers at B-Dienst in Berlin (until heavy bombing drove them out to the small village of Eberswalde) were reading most of the signals between the British Admiralty and its ships and convoys at sea.

This is not to diminish the achievements of the Bletchley people, which led to a series of individual victories from the Battle of Matapan to the Battle of North Cape, when the battlecruiser *Scharnhorst* was sunk. Harry Hinsley, who worked there himself – and wrote the definitive study of British intelligence in the Second World War – argued that cracking Enigma brought the war to an end at least a year sooner, because the U-boat threat had been comprehensively defeated at the start of 1944, allowing the necessary troops and material to be brought across the Atlantic to make D-Day possible.

There is no doubt about the crucial role that Bletchley played in the victory over the Nazis, and especially over the U-boats. But it is important to balance what we know of the bursts of individual brilliance with the systems and community effort of naval intelligence as a whole, and as it actually was – a day by day, hour by hour struggle by two sets of intelligence machines and, in particular, two sets of brilliant code breakers.

Part of the purpose of this book is to draw together that struggle when it reached its height, during that crucial month of May 1941 – when the very survival of Britain hung in the balance – to work out why one side managed by the skin of their teeth to develop the advantages that they could use eventually to defeat the other on the high seas....

Operation Primrose is available on Kindle from Endeavour Press and as a paperback from The Real Press.

Other books by David Boyle

Building Futures
Funny Money: In search of alternative cash
What is New Economics?
The Sum of our Discontent
The Tyranny of Numbers
The Money Changers
Numbers (with Anita Roddick)
Authenticity: Brands, Fakes, Spin and the Lust for
Real Life
Blondel's Song
Why London needs its own currency
News from Somewhere (*editor*)
The New Economics: A Bigger Picture (with
Andrew Simms)
Money Matters: Putting the eco into economics
The Wizard (fiction)
The Little Money Book
Eminent Corporations (with Andrew Simms)
Voyages of Discovery
The Human Element
What if money grew on trees (*editor*)
Broke: How to survive the middle class crisis
Give and Take (with Sarah Bird)
People Powered Prosperity (with Tony Greenham)

How to be English
The Piper (fiction)
Scandal
How to become a freelance writer

Other Endeavour Press titles
Leaves the World to Darkness (fiction)
Toward the Setting Sun
On the Eighth Day, God Created Allotments
The Age to Come
Unheard, Unseen: Submarine E14 and the
Dardanelles
Alan Turing: Unlocking the Enigma
Peace on Earth: The Christmas truce of 1914
Jerusalem: England's National Anthem
Rupert Brooke: England's Last Patriot
Operation Primrose
Before Enigma

CPSIA information can be obtained
at www.ICGtesting.com
Printed in the USA
LVHW111638250620
658989LV00001B/386

9 781533 131546